THE COMPLETE REFERENCE CHECKING HANDBOOK

THE COMPLETE REFERENCE CHECKING HANDBOOK

Smart, Fast, Legal Ways to Check Out Job Applicants

EDWARD C. ANDLER

AMACOM

American Management Association

New York • Atlanta • Boston • Chicago • Kansas City • San Francisco • Washington, D.C.
Brussels • Mexico City • Tokyo • Toronto

This publication is designed to provide accurate and authoritative
information in regard to the subject matter covered. It is sold with the
understanding that the publisher is not engaged in rendering legal,
accounting, or other professional service. If legal advice or other expert
assistance is required, the services of a competent professional person
should be sought.

Library of Congress Cataloging-in-Publication Data

Andler, Edward C.
      The complete reference checking handbook: smart, fast, legal ways
to check out job applicants / Edward C. Andler.
           p.   cm.
      Includes index.
      ISBN 0-8144-0405-7
      1. Employee screening—United States.   2. Employee selection—
United States.   3. Employment references—United States.
      I. Title.
      HF5549.5.E429A53   1998
      658.3'112—dc21   97-32352
                                                                        CIP

Printing number

10   9   8   7   6   5   4   3   2   1

To all the good people who are
being hurt because their
former employers won't say
anything nice about them.

Contents

Introduction

"You wouldn't buy a piece of machinery without knowing who else has used it, how often it breaks down, how fast it operates, or how well it fits with your other equipment. Yet we are constantly hiring people without finding out the answers to these basic questions."

Edward C. Andler

Smart hiring is crucial to business success today. Lying by job candidates shows no sign of tapering off despite a strong economy and job market. Recruiters estimate that about one-third of applicants lie to some degree about their backgrounds. Nearly twelve percent lie about education. Many exaggerate their job responsibilities and compensation. Others try to hide a job that didn't work out or a period of unemployment.

Employers and job applicants often view résumés differently. Companies see a résumé as a factual document. Job hunters see it as a marketing tool and thereby justify embellishing it. Many candidates lie because they know someone who got away with fudging and landed a good job. Most lies are put on a résumé to get a foot in the door or to get a leg up on the competition.

Now more than ever pre-employment selection must be done well. Hiring the wrong employee means putting high turnover, absenteeism, discipline problems, and theft on the payroll—with the resulting cost consequences to the company.

Turnover Is a Major Problem

Employee turnover would not be such a problem if the hiring practices of most companies today were effective, but such is not the case. Each year, American organizations spend an unbelievable amount of time, money, and energy on newly hired employees who do not work out and either leave on their own or are fired. In most instances, new employers have taken on previous employers' problems, which then come back to haunt them. Had the employer spent a little extra time and effort up front, and talking to the people who knew or worked with these applicants, far fewer bad hiring decisions would be made.

But the problem of ineffective hiring goes beyond the disturbingly high proportion of employees who either quit or are terminated after a relatively short time on the job. It extends to the millions of employees who do not leave but are marginal or mediocre workers who do only enough to get by. These marginal employees stay on the payroll but don't accomplish or produce nearly as much as well-fitted or highly motivated employees do. They are costly burdens to the organization that hired them.

The problem is further complicated by the growing legal restraints on firing, which make it much more difficult to get rid of an employee for any reason without being sued. The litigation rate for some employers and in some geographic areas is rising rapidly. I once heard the vice president and chief legal officer of a large company, speaking at the company's annual human resources conference, say that he was greatly concerned because the largest number of his open cases—with probably the largest potential legal costs—involved "wrongful discharge" lawsuits. He went on to explain that, in his opinion, all the discharge cases involved conduct and problems that should have been detected by good background checking at the time these persons were being considered. He said, with a nod of agreement from the top human resources officer, that his company had to start doing a better job up front.

Taking it easy up front and then clearing out the bad apples only after they have become your employees is just not a smart way of doing business. You should make a solid hiring decision and hire the best person for the job the first time.

There Has to Be a Better Way

Based on my experience, I am convinced that the vast majority of hiring mistakes can be prevented by checking job candidates' past behavior, and this is not that hard to do. That's why I have written this book. My purpose can be explained simply: I want to help you ensure that you're hiring the people best suited for your job openings and that you avoid major hiring mistakes through conducting effective background reviews.

I hope to do this in two ways. First, I will help you to see why we are where we are on this matter of not checking people out. Second, I will show you what can be done to get background information easily and quickly.

This book is written to be used. It is not a book on personnel theory or legal interpretations. I firmly believe that most, if not all, of the manuals on employment screening have been confusing and even frightening and, if anything, have made everyone more reluctant and impotent in this area. There is such a thing as bad training.

In this book, I focus on practical methods to help managers, supervisors, and professionals improve their ability to conduct background checks on prospective employees. Job seekers, too, may benefit from reading it, by better understanding the needs of hiring managers. The focus of this book is on technique, not theory; on action, not admonishment; on the practical reasons, not the psychological explanations, as to why people do the things they do. In other words, I want to empower you to do a better job, not confuse you so that you become less effective. My goal is to provide new and powerful ideas that will enable you to become immediately more proficient in this area. This book offers the ways and means by which background checking can be improved.

Good people who are seeking new positions lose out when no one wants to say anything about them. Of course, as companies withhold information, they receive less too. This creates problems for candidates in trying to find the right job and for companies in trying to hire the right people. There is little disagreement that information is needed when trying to determine whether the person is going to be a good fit.

Where the Author Comes From

During my thirty years of nationwide staffing experience, I estimate that I have personally looked at more than 250,000 résumés, read about 60,000 of them, interviewed more than 10,000 people, and conducted more than 3,000 background checks on individual candidates, with more than 10,000 separate reference contacts.

Since leaving corporate management, I have looked at the employment process as it is practiced in this country and wondered why we keep making the same mistakes. Fortunately, I have been able to stand back, get a much better view, and see that new thinking is definitely needed in this field. I am now devoting my time to applying new techniques to the process of background screening and evaluation for a diverse list of corporate clients. I have given special seminars on this subject throughout the United States. This training covers highly effective ways to cut screening time and improve results, whether it's carried out by staff or line employees. Hundreds of companies are now using these techniques.

If there is a single message to this book, it is: Put up your antennae and be open to fresh ideas. Review your present thinking and practices regarding hiring, then combine them with these new ideas—and you will greatly enhance your chances of choosing the right person for each job you must fill. I truly believe that no organization in America will be successful in assembling a competitive work force in today's difficult times unless it turns to innovative, nontraditional strategies for selecting the best available workers.

I have not been content to lament the decline of the employment game and let it go at that. I have attempted to give specific and positive solutions. Some are simple and practical; others are somewhat revolutionary. Change for the better is possible once everybody has enough information with which to work. I want to put common sense back into checking out candidates. So, let's be creative, roll up our sleeves, and get to work to hire the right people for our organization.

Why a New Book on Hiring?

This is by no means the first book on the subject of hiring. I make no claim to originality on that score. However, thumbing through previously published volumes on the subject, I noticed a major defect running through many of them. Though each explained the steps involved in hiring (some more lucidly than others), none showed the reader *how* to check references.

This book is designed to change the way you see the subject. If you apply my principles, you will hire the right people. It's an action manual. You can utilize these principles and techniques every day. Refer often to the book. Check back to see if you're on track. Don't worry, I'm right behind you.

Seven Fallacies of Reference Checking

Before proceeding, let's examine seven common fallacies about checking out applicants.

1. *One in ten job candidates exaggerates or embellishes his work history.* That figure is actually much higher. The latest surveys indicate that about one in three candidates will embellish his background.
2. *About 20 percent of executive applicants have their résumés written for them.* Actually, 75 percent or more of executive-level résumés have been written (or substantially rewritten) by someone else.
3. *To minimize your company's legal risks, you shouldn't reveal information about a present or past employee when contacted by another potential employer.* Virtually every attorney recommends that employers get as much information as possible before hiring someone. It makes no sense, therefore, not to offer assistance when contacted by other employers—as long as you do it properly so as to minimize your organization's legal exposure.
4. *Checking references is mainly to see if a person is lying.* Checking for truthfulness is actually secondary to determining a candidate's past job performance and overall competence level.
5. *References given by candidates aren't valuable because they're usually friends who have been told what to say.* Good questioning will give you important insights into the applicant. Personal references are also a place to start in gathering the names of other people who know the applicant.
6. *If you don't want to jeopardize the job of someone who's currently employed, there's not much you can do to find out about her.* There

are always other people with whom you can speak. Individuals who have recently left the company, clients or customers, co-workers close to the candidate who know what's going on, and company retirees are all sources of information.

7. *Asking a candidate to clarify unclear or confusing information that surfaced during your background check is legally dangerous.* Clarifying confusing information is really the only fair thing to do with someone you still consider a viable candidate.

Hopefully, when you finish this book, you will have no trouble agreeing with these explanations and conclusions.

Part I

Dishonesty—A Major Business and Social Problem

1

It's a Whole New World Out There

Suffice it to say that a high number of job seekers today are willing to modify who they are, what they can do, or what they have done in order to find new employment. If you haven't been checking out your employees before you hire them, you can figure that possibly a third of the people working for you gained their jobs by creatively presenting their backgrounds and capabilities to your hiring "expert." Lying on résumés, the problems of deception and exaggeration in general, have been compounded by the difficulties human resources people have in checking references.

Surveying the Problem

During my discussions over the years with hundreds of hiring managers, these managers readily admitted that they make hiring decisions without having on hand all the information they need. They feel they don't get adequate information on violent or bizarre behavior, personality traits, work habits, reason for leaving previous employers, human relations skills, past level of performance, and salary history.

In past years numerous studies have been conducted on résumé distortion. The amount of misrepresentation reported by reliable surveys clearly indicates that the problem has been rising steadily over the years. In 1997, misrepresentation was reported to be approximately 36 percent, which is about the same result as shown in a 1991 survey; in 1981 it was about 23 percent; and in 1979 it was only 17 percent. This trend can be seen clearly in Exhibit 1-1.

Past surveys indicated that résumé deception was a growing trend. Today's surveys seem to show that falsifying one's credentials has become so common that it's now accepted as a fact of life. Clearly, there is measurable evidence that dishonesty is now a very significant factor that must be dealt with by today's employment professionals. There is a growing realization that job market lying has gone too far.

Our Changing Society

This trend is showing up throughout society. Employee theft and shoplifting have created a significant increase in retail shrinkage over the past decade. Losses from theft keep rising despite retailer's increased investment in security systems to protect themselves. Many use a two-tag sys-

Exhibit 1-1. Rising incidence of résumé distortion, 1979–1998.

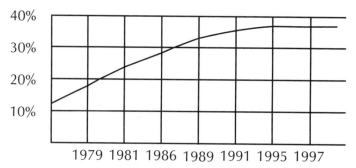

tem—a visible hard tag and an invisible second-ary device—to deter thieves. More stores are filing charges against shoplifters, often using video-taped evidence to get convictions. Even modern pay phones have been modified for today's world with such antivandalism features as steel-coated cords, one-piece receivers, and "no-pick" locks.

The point is that we have a serious dishon-esty problem at practically all levels of society, and we are responding to it. Personally, we are placing security devices in our own homes and automobiles to protect our most prized posses-sions. New methods and equipment are coming on the market every day to safeguard ourselves and our property. Security has become big busi-ness.

The Ostrich Reaction to Dishonesty

On the other hand, in the area of employment screening, where we know full well that there is also a very serious problem, little—and in most cases, nothing—is being done to protect employ-ers. The legal community and human resources professionals have essentially thrown up their hands and taken the position that there just isn't much that can be done about job applicants' dis-honesty. The very people who are supposed to spot dishonesty in job seekers have allowed, al-most encouraged, this to happen. We all know this to be true from the few calls that we receive from other employers requesting information about our former employees. The result is a vi-cious form of recycling: Employers are simply exchanging the marginal or poor performers among themselves.

I call this the "ostrich reaction" to the major problem in hiring—dishonesty by job applicants. Like the ostrich, we hide our heads in the sand and try to avoid the danger by refusing to face it. In the process, we have removed the major deterrent to dishonest claims by people applying for employment.

When we do not check out the information job applicants give us, we provide an opportunity for questionable individuals to take advantage of the situation and lie to us. Eventually, even the honest job seekers will resort to falsification just to keep up with the dishonest ones who are getting by on false pretenses.

As the employment director of a large banking institution in a major city told me, "In the banking business in our town, we are all keeping our best tellers. What we are doing, however, is exchanging the poor ones among ourselves. I want to get out of this loop." When you stop to think about it, it doesn't make much sense to fire a poor employee and then turn right around and hire another bad one. Yet when you fail to take the time to check out those you hire, that's exactly what you are doing. If you hire someone else's problem, you're right back where you started. That's precisely why many companies are never able to upgrade their work force.

In my business of providing third-party reference-checking services for client companies throughout the country, I have found that about 15 percent of the job candidates we check out do not get hired because of the information we uncover. Just think how nice it would be to be able to spot these individuals yourself and not bring them on board.

In my reference checking practice, I have found that when I report to an employer that a candidate has falsified his or her background in some way, the employer is glad to have discovered the discrepancy in advance of offering that person employment. I frequently hear comments like, "They just never learn that they can't get by lying to us." The problem is that job seekers have learned that they *can* lie and probably get away with it most of the time. This just happened to be a rare case when someone was caught.

Stretching the Truth Too Far

To see how distortion occurs in the job market, let's look at the case of a fictional sales candidate (call him Fred) who, over the last ten years, has been a typical average performer with his current employer. At year-end, Fred has consistently ranked in the middle among the company's twenty-plus-member sales force. Some years he was a little above average; other years he was slightly below the middle mark. Now, like most salespeople, Fred had some very good months when he was near the top in sales. He has also won some special sales contests and opened a number of good accounts. Over the long haul, though, the middle has been his place among the group. He is a reliable, but not an exceptional, sales employee. Fred knows this, and his current employer is well aware of his predictable level of performance.

Fred has now decided to look for new employment, and he can present his previous employment record in a number of ways. Obviously, he can be very straightforward and honest and tell it like it is. But, let's say he decides to "fluff" his background somewhat as he goes out for interviews.

Fred tells a prospective new employer that he was one of his company's best salesmen. Now this is not really false, because there were times when he was near the top. In other words, he has conveniently exaggerated his past performance in a way that makes him look good. This is probably a fairly normal occurrence.

Now, let's say Fred tells an employer that he was so competent that he was singled out to train other sales representatives. The fact of the matter is that the entire sales force was brought in every Friday from 7:00 A.M. to 9:00 P.M. for refresher training, and each sales representative was assigned various subjects on a routine basis to cover for about an hour. Fred, like all the other members of the sales group, was periodically given a topic to cover. He was not singled out for his expertise, as he would like the potential employer to believe, but was merely used as a trainer at times as a way to fulfill the training need. Fred has deliberately misrepresented his role in order to get this employer to think that he was so good he was personally selected to train the other salespeople, which in fact is not really the case at all. I believe you would agree that this is a much more serious distortion of the facts.

Now, let's say Fred tells a potential employer that he was in the top 10 percent of his company's sales force last year—an outright lie. I believe all of us would consider this to be a clear and obvious attempt to get us to believe that he is something he is not.

If you discovered the truth—which you can do—you will probably react in a fairly predictable way. In the first case of exaggeration, you may still hire Fred, depending on how everything else looks. In the second instance, where there was obvious misrepresentation, you would mostly likely lose interest in him as a candidate. And, in the third situation, where Fred lied to you, you would definitely call it off.

The Bottom Line on Hiring Today

Bad news usually costs a lot less if you get it sooner rather than later. What is the real effect of exaggeration, misrepresentation, and lying by job candidates? As with buying a product or service that's not what it's advertised to be, you're not getting what you think you're getting. The lesson to be learned is probably best summed up in an old gambler's proverb, "Always trust your fellow man—and always cut the cards." Let's face it, a candidate eager for a job is under tremendous pressure to say whatever it takes to get the job.

There is no law or requirement that job applicants have to tell you their flaws, or even be truthful. It's the employer's task to find the distortions or lies.

It's time for Real World 101. Our hiring practices must be based on reality, not wishful thinking. The airline industry faced the problem of hijacking a number of years ago and now checks all passenger luggage. It's time for employers to face their problem and start checking who they are bringing on board.

Change can creep up on us and we don't even realize it's happening. It's a new age with new challenges for businesses to face and solve. For those of you who are your company's "gatekeepers," with responsibility for keeping the wrong people from being hired, there has to be a way to solve this problem. Fortunately, there are creative measures that can be taken.

2

When the Candidate Has the Advantage

The scale now dips toward the applicant in the current job market. Motivated job seekers can draw from innumerable services, specialists, and products to hone their interviewing skills. There is literally a whole industry out there to help job seekers, including career counseling or outplacement assistance, professional résumé writers, search firms and employment agencies, to say nothing of the numerous books, audio and visual tapes on how to find a job, and even computer programs to track them through their entire job search. Let's look more closely at each of these and see how they can help and, in many cases, really "polish up" an applicant.

Career Counseling and Outplacement

Career counseling has been around a long time. Most of us probably went to career counselors in high school or college. Frequently counselors are teachers who may not really know or be experienced in the business world. If reasonably competent, however, counselors can help point job seekers in the right direction.

Outplacement comes in two forms: retail and company-paid. You have probably seen advertisements for retail career planning (or management or development or transition) firms in big-city newspapers and phone books. Many firms of this type have come and gone, some with dubious reputations for professional conduct and results. These firms cater to those who are looking for jobs or want to make a career change. They emphasize their career marketing services for moving candidates through the job market using planning and personal assistance programs. They try to find candidates who are finding their search too time-consuming or unproductive—and charge a substantial fee to help them.

Company-paid outplacement firms are retained by corporations to help terminated employees land new jobs. They start out by trying to minimize the trauma associated with termination and then develop a structured program to guide employees in their job search. They usually prepare résumés and give personalized attention to each individual with follow-up guidance as needed. Their goal is to reduce the time needed to locate a new position. Their fees, which vary depending on the level of service provided, are based on a prearranged understanding with the last employer.

Both retail and company-paid services follow a basically similar outline that involves explaining the realities of the job market, writing an effective résumé, developing techniques to generate interviews, targeting industries and organizations, and helping with letter-writing campaigns. Many also provide interview training with actual practice on videotape. Obviously, a good firm can be a tremendous help to job candidates in understanding and tackling the tough chore of finding the right new job.

Résumé-Preparation Services

A résumé says basically: Here's where I have worked, here's what I did, and here's how good I was at it. A whole industry has been built around the preparation and production of the mythical "perfect" résumé.

Résumé-writing services and help, both formal and informal, now abound everywhere. Even some Sears stores have offered résumé preparation as one of their services. A high percentage of résumés are either entirely written or at least rewritten for job hunters. At one time, a résumé indicated a candidate's writing ability and knowledge of grammar. That's not true anymore. The higher the job level, the greater is the chance that the résumé was prepared professionally. At the executive level, almost all résumés have a professional touch.

Experts in the employment field advise that the primary purpose of a résumé is to get the writer of it an interview. After all, a résumé initially gets examined for only about twenty seconds before a decision is made whether or not to consider the candidate. It is in the interview that the candidate must sell himself or herself to get a job. The résumé should therefore be succinct and to the point—like a good product advertisement. It should contain just enough information to convince the employer to call the person in for an interview. Unfortunately, many candidates don't realize this and create long and rambling documents that are actually boring and self-defeating. A candidate is ahead of the competition if the résumé does nothing to unsell his or her candidacy.

You might ask, so what if a résumé is puffed up a little bit? Perhaps you believe that it's all right if the résumé attempts to present the candidate in the best light. The problem is that the résumé is the candidate's script and, if it is exaggerated or falsified, that message has to be carried out through the entire hiring process.

Job-Hunting Books, Tapes, and Computer Programs

There are a lot of books, audiotapes, and videotapes on the market that tell you how to do well in the job search and succeed in finding new employment. Most of them are good and offer sound advice to the perplexed, confused, or even desperate job seeker. Goodness knows, looking for a job is a rough situation for most people and even quite frightening for many. Therefore, any help or encouragement they can get is desirable and needed.

More and more, today's emphasis is on the use of computers and on-line databases that match job seekers to positions and recruiters to job seekers, or allow an individual to scan openings that may be of interest. There are a variety of computerized databases that give applicants the opportunity to research companies or industries quickly and comprehensively according to their size, revenues, product, location, or any other meaningful combination. Such comprehensive resources provide ready information to job seekers and reduce the amount of time ordinarily spent on researching target companies and trying to figure out what they want. Through database resource companies, it is now possible to pinpoint the person to whom you should send your résumé. Thus, more time and attention can be spent on actually trying to capture the position sought, and this further tips the whole process toward the applicant.

Search Firms and Employment Agencies

Talking about the advantages candidates have in the job market wouldn't be complete without mentioning the way search firms and employment agencies go out of their way to help candidates. Let's face it, search firms and agencies have one purpose—to place people in new jobs and get paid for it. Although these services may extol their desire to match the right people with the right job, the bottom line is that they have to place people somewhere to pay their bills and stay in business.

The first step these firms take is to identify their candidate's strong points and then sell prospective employers on seeing this candidate. They usually do a better job than a job hunter would have done on his or her own behalf, because most people aren't that comfortable bragging about themselves. They then prepare the person for the interview by telling him what the company, the job, and the interviews are like. They will sometimes go into great detail on what questions to anticipate and how to answer them. They may even advise the candidate on the idiosyncrasies and preferences of the company's interviewers, so the candidate will be better prepared to handle them or even to take control of them. An employment consultant at one of the nation's largest placement firms told me: "I may spend up to two hours coaching any candidate on how to beat the interview and win the job. I want him to be the one who's selected. That's how I earn my living."

I have seen written summaries from employment firms that were really "cooked"; that is, they omitted important and unfavorable items of information, or so cleverly disguised negative points that they didn't appear to be the problems they really were. In fact, I have even seen summaries in which dates of employment had been moved around to make a candidate's record look as if she had been continuously employed during her career, which was definitely not the case.

Appearances May Be Misleading

The candidate who stands before an interviewer is at his or her very best. He or she probably has on a new suit or dress, has spruced up for the occasion, and is making a real effort to be a pleasant and likable human being. We have all had to look for a job and know that this is what to do. We want to put our best foot forward. Someone who smokes, for example, knows almost instinctively not to light up a cigarette during an interview, even though he is an inveterate smoker who normally can't go fifteen minutes without smoking.

A client once told me about a receptionist she had hired who completely fooled her. The company, which is housed in a beautiful building with very modern and impressive offices, is an elite firm and wanted to project that image quickly to visitors. The manager twice interviewed one young lady who seemed to have it all. She was pretty, well-dressed, and well-spoken. She looked like a perfect fit for the reception desk in the company's exclusive surroundings. But, when she came to work the first day, the staff could hardly believe their eyes. Her hair and makeup were almost outlandish, her clothes were too trendy, and her speech and actions were completely different from what she had projected in the interview. The personnel specialist and the manager responsible for hiring her immediately went into conference on what to do. When the company chairman came through the reception area and did a double take, he immediately sought out those responsible for hiring this immature young girl for such a visible position.

To make a long story short, she had borrowed both outfits she wore when being interviewed; a friend had helped her with her makeup and hair so that she would project a more businesslike image; and she even had some special coaching on how to speak and act in a more mature manner. She portrayed the role very well and got the job, but in fact she was a very young girl who didn't have a business wardrobe and really didn't want to conform to the style of a professional environment. It was all a facade. They released her and started their search all over again.

This happens every day. It's the way the game is played. Men are told to shave off their beards if they have one, get a haircut, wear a conservative suit, shine their shoes, leave off vulgar rings, etc. Women are told to adopt a businesslike appearance and demeanor, to wear only the most conservative jewelry, and are given other pertinent advice suitable to the level and type of position for which they are applying.

The most common pitfall recruiters face is to be dazzled by personality. Even top recruiters may confuse an applicant's interview skills with the skills he or she will need on the job. We are all vulnerable to charmers.

Many candidates, deliberately or unknowingly, describe themselves as the person they would like to be, rather than as they really are. As a former employment director for a major company, I can't count the times we were fooled by an applicant. I recall hiring a director of public relations for the company who seemed to have all the qualifications—plus some—for the position, and his references checked out fine. I noticed on the day he started that he was very nervous and couldn't even sign all the enrollment forms. He explained that he had first day jitters and also that he had taken some medication, which was making him even more agitated. It turned out he had developed a severe drinking problem and was quickly sliding downhill. From the start he was unreliable and unpredictable and after three months was released by the company.

I have heard numerous applicants for hourly plant work brag about their good work habits and steady attendance. After being hired, sometimes without a background check, they start doing poor work and come in late or are absent too often. I recall one individual we fired for poor attendance who insisted he was helping to care for his sick grandmother who was dying of a rare disease. This seemed noble and good, until we found out his grandmother passed away ten years earlier. It's amazing how many employees have a sick grandmother. Maybe reference checking should include finding out the number and health of an applicant's grandparents.

Anyone who has done a lot of hiring can relate similar stories of candidates who shine during the interview and then, when hired, display poor work habits or a bad attitude. After all, an employer would not knowingly hire someone who wasn't going to work out in the job. Applicants know this, and almost by reflex, paint a glowing picture of themselves in order to get the job.

What it all comes down to is that what you see and hear when you interview someone is not always what you get in the long run. The whole hiring situation often becomes a big game of fooling the interviewer. Fortunately, you can find out what the person is really like if you take the time and effort to go back and talk to the people who have known or worked with the applicant in the past. The information is there if you will just seek it out.

The Truth About Salaries

Perhaps most job candidates overstate their compensation to some degree. Salary deception has become epidemic in part because individuals believe it's one way to get ahead. Moreover it's relatively easy for job seekers to lie because few businesses bother to verify past salaries. Employers don't want to offend job candidates. They are more concerned with getting the right person than with whether they are offering too much.

Pay deception is a problem employers have to deal with every day. Many job candidates believe that dishonesty does pay. Some applicants fudge their pay simply because they think it's standard procedure. People in the job market ask each other: "How much are you going to tell them you make?" It has become part of the cat-and-mouse game that goes on during the interview process.

Unfortunately, too many companies rely primarily on a candidate's current pay, or what they think it is, rather than on the job level itself. That's all right if it's on the high side. But if a person is underpaid, that tends to get perpetrated in the next job, as companies unfairly take advantage of the low starting point. This is a large part of the reason women and minorities are paid less than their white male counterparts are.

Some people rationalize their deception by including nonsalary benefits in their pay figure. Candidates can truthfully give a wide range of figures when asked about compensation. They can offer a summary of these benefits and then try to negotiate. But in some cases, job hunters try to land fatter salaries by fabricating titles or college degrees.

The picture is starting to change. More companies are starting to check out applicants' pay history. Some verify salary levels by demanding W-2 income forms from job seekers. But even well-crafted plans aren't foolproof. Many job candidates refuse to produce W-2 forms. And, let's face it, there are ways to come up with a fake W-2 form. Again, the employer always has to be on guard.

3

It's Time to Regain Control

Don't lose control of the hiring process, because if you do, the candidate will take over. There are two basic reasons job candidates lie.

1. To avoid something that will lower their standing in the interviewer's eyes (in order not to lose out to the other applicants)
2. To appear more competent and valuable to the firm (that is, create a higher compensation need)

Candidates know instinctively that they are competing against other job seekers for a particular job. Depending on the position and the number of people competent and willing to fill it, the degree of competition varies. In any case, the person chosen will somehow have to win over everyone else. For all practical purposes, coming in second is no better than coming in last. It's serious business and we all know this. So, for many applicants, being successful means bending the facts to be the victor. Exhibit 3-1 shows specifically what job seekers may do to win a job.

Lying About Degrees

There are real-world reasons for fudging the facts or even lying outright when looking for a job. In

Exhibit 3-1. How and why applicants misrepresent themselves.

Educational Background
- ▶ Degree(s) never attained—to appear well-educated
- ▶ School(s) not attended—for prestige value
- ▶ Outside course work never started/completed —to appear industrious
- ▶ Participation in made-up campus activities—to appear well-rounded

Employment History
- ▶ Stretch dates of employment—to cover periods of unemployment
- ▶ Omit certain employers—to hide unsatisfactory employment record
- ▶ List company that is out of business or has been absorbed—so checking is difficult or impossible

Salary and Job Title
- ▶ Inflate previous salary—to create higher compensation need
- ▶ Embellish job title—to appear more successful

Expertise and Achievements
- ▶ Indicate supervisory/management positions not held—to reflect leadership ability
- ▶ Embellish duties and responsibilities—to appear more experienced and successful
- ▶ Indicate performance levels not attained—to appear more competent
- ▶ Exaggerate results achieved (sales, profits, programs)—to appear more successful

Self-Employment
- ▶ List self-employment or personal consulting—to cover a period of unemployment or a job that didn't work out
- ▶ Exaggerate self-employed accomplishments—to appear successful

Exhibit 3-1. (Continued)

Criminal Record
- ▶ Omit convictions—to remove any doubt regarding honesty or reliability
- ▶ Downplay past record—to divert attention from personal problems

References
- ▶ List well-known or important people—to impress employer
- ▶ Program references to say the right things—to cover misrepresentation

the area of education, for example, surveys repeatedly show that a college degree greatly increases one's earning power. When the median income of college-educated men and women is compared with that of high-school educated men and women, we can see that college graduates have a higher income. Is it any wonder then that someone who didn't finish (or even attend) college will show a degree on her résumé—especially when she thinks it will never be checked?

There has been a noticeable increase in the number of job applicants who lie about having a degree. Hard times have created an unprecedented level of competition for jobs, and many nongraduates feel compelled to say that they have a degree in order to stand a chance.

I have seen this in my own reference checking practice. Today, about one out of twelve will report a bogus degree. Among sales candidates, about 1 out of 8 is guilty of claiming a degree not earned. University officials in Texas have warned employers in their state that "academic fraud" has assumed epidemic proportions, especially in professions that require an advanced education such as health care, law, and engineering.

Unfortunately, the majority of companies do not check degrees prior to hiring employees. This lack of diligence by employers has fueled the problem, as job seekers realized they could succeed at fabricating their level of education.

I recall some near-ludicrous stories from my own recent experience. In one case, a male applicant reported he had graduated from the University of Colorado in Denver, where he played four years of varsity football. Of course, the football team is in Boulder and the applicant had never gone there. In another instance, a woman applicant claimed she had graduated from the University of Connecticut, where she was president of her sorority. In truth, she had gone to the school only one year and was never in a sorority.

I have uncovered phony degrees among candidates from executives to hourly applicants. People without a college or high school degree will blatantly indicate on their résumés and employment applications that they have a certain degree, and will even include the year of graduation. Many hiring officials falsely assume that because someone spells it out on paper the information must be true. In my opinion, this is a serious disservice to those who have actually completed their education, usually at a considerable expenditure of effort and money.

Probably the most outlandish claim to a college degree I have encountered involved a vice president of human resources who was being considered for a similar role with a larger company. After an extensive effort to verify the bachelor and master's degrees he claimed to have, it was obvious he only attended college for two years and, of course, never graduated. The alarming aspect was that he sat on the advisory board of the College of Business of a major state university where he was listed as having an M.B.A. degree from another state university. Also, he frequently gave talks to students at the school on the value and importance of their M.B.A. program.

When I advised my client that the candidate did not have the academic credentials he claimed, they were shocked and eventually turned him down for the position, explaining that they had selected someone else. Even though they were closely affiliated with the university where he held an advisory role, they elected not to tell school officials what had been discovered because they thought it would just stir up the waters with them in the middle.

You have to wonder how many executives and other key people don't have the level of credentials they claim. Although it is probably not a major problem, it is still more prevalent than we care to admit.

Another bizarre situation occurred when I was checking out a salesman for a large chemical company. I called the school where the candidate said he had received a B.S. degree in chemistry. They informed me that he had attended for two years, but did not graduate. I called the company and told them what I had learned. The employment manager said there must be some mistake because he was looking at a copy of the applicant's transcript which the candidate had faxed to him. He faxed the transcript copy to me which I sent in turn to the registrar at the school. The registrar called and explained that the top one-third of the transcript showing the candidate's name and other information was correct; however the bottom two-thirds were from another student's transcript, in fact, one who graduated with very good grades. What the candidate had done was to paste his I.D. information on the top to make it look like his transcript. It was a clever composite reproduction. Even the embossed school seal showed on the bottom of the document. Because it was faxed, the glued-together document looked like the real thing.

Not checking someone's reported degree is just asking to be lied to. Even more important, it can lead to hiring an underqualified person or someone who will continue to lie as an employee. Applicants usually know which employers aren't checking them out, so these firms get lied to the most.

It is very easy to confirm attendance and degrees at most U.S. and foreign colleges simply by calling the registrar's office of the school. With few exceptions you can verify school attendance and degrees over the phone, and this procedure usually takes no more than four to eight minutes to complete. Try calling your own school to see how easy it is to get this information.

Schools should provide this service as a way of recognizing their graduates, and as a way of keeping phonies from getting a "free education" from the school. A few schools won't give the information by phone, which I believe is a terrible mistake because the word gets out and dishonest applicants use that school as an easy mark, a result that is very unfair to the real graduates.

Most employers rate about a C minus in checking out their future employees. I suggest starting your reference checking with the education claimed. If you find a discrepancy there, you may not want to proceed any further. If someone tells you that he graduated from the University of Notre Dame in South Bend, Ohio, beware.

Career History

Some job candidates, in an attempt to hide the gaps in their employment history, "sketch" the dates during which they were actually employed. In my reference checking I have found candidates who were actually incarcerated, seriously ill, or in drug rehabilitation, which they chose to cover up. In other cases they just decided to take a long time off or simply could not find new employment. Rather than be questioned and have to explain their absence from the work world, they chose to drop this time from their résumé or employment application, in some cases by falsifying the actual dates they were employed at certain places. To combat this, many employers now ask applicants to list periods of unemployment on the employment application form as a way of forcing candidates to be honest when recalling their work history. See Exhibit 3-2.

The "X" Factor

What has happened in the job market can best be seen by examining the "X" Factor, shown in Ex-

Exhibit 3-2. Example of an unemployment record.

List all periods of two weeks duration or more when you
were not working.

FROM		TO		REASON
Mo.	Yr.	Mo.	Yr.	
Mo.	Yr.	Mo.	Yr.	
Mo.	Yr.	Mo.	Yr.	
Mo.	Yr.	Mo.	Yr.	

hibit 3-3. The "X" Factor is simply two lines. The
control line represents the amount of checking by
the employer; the reaction line is the amount of
lying by applicants. What it shows is that as the
amount of checking decreases, the amount of
lying increases.

For whatever reason—probably legal interpretations and equal employment considerations—the amount of reference checking by
employers throughout the United States has been
steadily declining. Those candidates who are inclined to be dishonest have sensed this and taken
advantage of it. The problem is that candidates
who would prefer to be honest in presenting
themselves know that unless they too embellish
who they are, they may get left behind. The whole
situation has resulted in a serious and increasing
mess in today's job market.

Now let's look at how this phenomenon af-
fects individual companies. You can bet that if

Exhibit 3-3. The "X" factor at work.

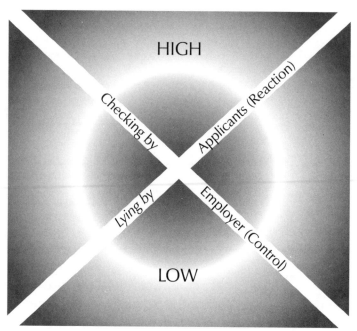

your company has let slip the amount of background verification it does, people in the job market are probably aware of it and are taking advantage of the situation. Word gets out quickly as to where you can go and say what you want and get by with it, and where you can't.

I tell people who attend my seminars on employment screening that while they are sleeping, applicants are thinking up ways to fool them. I relay a story that actually happened to me many years ago when I was a personnel manager at a large manufacturing plant in the Los Angeles area. We had an employee working in the plant who seriously hurt his back doing heavy lifting. When I took him to the company doctor for

X-rays, the doctor told me that this employee, who had been with us about three months, had really hurt himself. He also advised that the employee had a deformed back and should not be working for us, much less doing heavy lifting. I reminded the doctor that he had given this person a pre-employment physical, which included a back X-ray, and he hadn't told us not to hire him at that time. He said "Oh-oh" and started comparing medical records. It turned out that the employee had arranged for someone else (25 pounds heavier and 5 inches taller) to take his physical for him, yet no one had caught it. To make a long story short, we immediately fired him, although he was given workers' compensation because of his injury.

After this incident, we immediately inaugurated a companywide procedure requiring applicants to sign a health questionnaire at the employment office and then countersign it at the doctor's office. Using driver's licenses to compare the signature and photograph is another good way to double-check who you are really working with.

Dishonest candidates can be smart and clever people, and they can thwart the employment process in strange and alarming ways. Unfortunately, too many dishonest candidates are taking advantage of the system, and even the honest ones are forced to be devious to keep up with them.

Pre-Employment Considerations

The need to check out those we are hiring has never been greater. There are three basic types of

problem candidates that employers must be able
to spot:

1. *The underqualified*—those who simply
    don't have the background, knowledge, or
    skills to be able to function in today's com-
    plex job categories
2. *People who are burned out*—those who have
    stayed in some job area too long and are
    tired and worn out. They need to get out
    of their old line of work and into some-
    thing new.
3. *The emotionally unstable*—those who are
    alcoholic, drug-dependent, or subject to
    some intractable emotional problem.

The problem is that most candidates don't
see or want to see that they are underqualified,
burned out, or no longer emotionally fit for the
type of work they are doing. Even if they have
experienced troubles in their careers that clearly
point to their not being well-suited to their work,
they continue to seek out jobs in the same line of
work.

A couple of actual cases come to mind:

A credit manager in a large manufacturing company
was fired for general indifference and lack of interest in
his work. He had started out many years before as a credit
analyst and progressed upward into credit management.
He really didn't enjoy processing requests for credit and
the large amount of administration connected with it, and
it was obvious that he was just hanging on for the gener-
ous benefits and retirement the company offered. The
company saw his bad attitude and low level of performance and asked him to leave. What kind of new position
did he look for? You guessed it—credit management.

A sales manager had been an outstanding sales representative prior to being promoted into sales management. However, he had lost his zip and interest and didn't do well in everyday sales administration. He had developed a bad drinking problem that was beginning to affect his health, family, and general well-being. He was let go and was on the job market looking for employment as—you guessed it—a sales manager.

A hiring mismatch is harmful in many ways. It takes a heavy psychic toll in stress and unhappiness on the individual, which can be transmitted to his or her family and friends. Certainly, other employees notice and feel the impact of someone who is not up to doing the job. In fact, they are the first to notice and to be affected by substandard job performance. Finally, an employer's business image, productivity, and even profits can be seriously affected by employees who are not able or willing to do their jobs properly.

Let's end this discussion on a humorous note. Even the best of us don't tell the truth all the time. The story goes that a minister told his congregation that the following week he would preach on lying. He asked them to read the Chapter 17 of the Gospel of St. Mark in the meantime. The next Sunday he asked how many had done the reading he had assigned. Several hands went up. "I see," said the minister. "You are the very people I want to reach. There is no Chapter 17 in St. Mark's Gospel."

The Honesty/Competency Scale

Whether we realize it or not, we are consciously or subconsciously trying to determine two factors when we screen job candidates. We want to find out how honest they are being with us, and we want to be able to predict how competent they will be on the job. Exhibit 3-4, the Honesty/Competency Scale, is always a real eye-opener to those attending my public and private seminars on employment screening.

A candidate would always like for us to believe that he is the ideal person for the job opening, that he is being totally honest, and that he is a top performer in his field. We know from Psychology 101 in college that people fall along a bell curve in all aspects of their personality or other characteristics. There are a few people at the extreme ends of the curve, which means that they are either very good or very poor in that attribute.

Exhibit 3-4. The Honesty/Competency Scale.

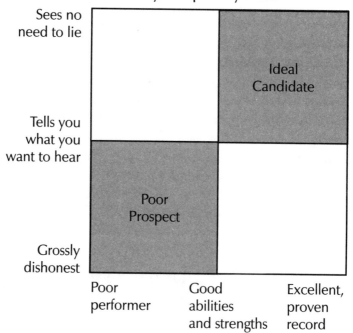

However, the vast majority fall into that great middle group of the average, or slightly above or below average. Therefore, among a group of candidates interviewed for a position, each person will fall somewhere along a spectrum of talents and abilities.

When we look at the Honesty Scale in Exhibit 3-4, we find that there are some applicants who see no need to be anything but totally honest. The vast majority, however, will generally tell you what you want to hear. If you are interviewing a programmer and you ask her if she has ever been involved in payroll programming, chances are she will quickly recall a situation in which she was involved in this area of computerization, telling you what you have signaled you want to hear. Or let's take a more personal situation. Let's say you are somewhat concerned about whom your teenage son is associating with, and ask, "Are those good boys you are spending your time around?" Picking up on your cue, he will probably answer, "Sure, they are. Why, Billy's dad is a minister and Joey's dad is a doctor," replying with what he knows you want to hear. He took your cue and gave you the reassurance you wanted.

On the Competency Scale of Exhibit 3-4, there are a few people who are proven top performers. Then there are those who are chronically poor performers, some of whom do not even realize that they are at this low level. Most people, however, fall into the generally average category of performance. No matter what the job level or category—executives, technicians, or street sweepers—there are top performers, average performers, and low performers. When presidents of the United States leave office, what do they worry about? They wonder if they will go down in history as great presidents, average ones, or poor ones.

There are top performers in every area or occupation. I remember reading about the top bulldozer operator in the country as determined by the annual National Truck and Equipment Rodeo competition. Friends of mine who are airline pilots tell me that they can sit next to another pilot with whom they have never flown and in minutes be able to tell how good a pilot the other one is. Think of this scale even for the carpenter who is going to build a porch on your house. Checking out how good someone is can apply to many areas of our lives even outside the workplace.

Management's View of Employment

Executives, managers, and staff members in organizations throughout the country invariably tell me that they check the references of prospective employees who are applying for jobs with their company most of the time. Middle managers, who are closer to what's actually going on, say that the references of their job candidates get checked about 75 percent of the time. However, the staff personnel actually responsible for doing the checking will admit that references get checked in only about 50 to 60 percent of the cases, and even then it's not always done very thoroughly.

The point is that management knows that the backgrounds of those hired by the company should be checked. It's just good business sense. The problem is that down on the working level it's a different story. The whole process of check-ing out job applicants gets shortchanged or is not done at all.

The problem, as we shall see, is that it is too burdensome to check references the way we have been led to believe it should be done. There just isn't enough time or a sufficient member of peo-ple to chase down references in today's compa-nies, where the hiring staffs are leaner and busier than they have ever been before, possibly because of major downsizing in the company.

Panning for Gold

Pyrite, a mineral that is light yellow with a metal-lic luster, was often mistaken for real gold during the gold rush years. It fooled enough prospectors to inspire its nickname, "fool's gold." To be sure of what they had, the prospectors would have it assayed.

Unfortunately, many interviewers have been similarly fooled by job candidates who gave the appearance and impression of being the real thing. However, under close examination through background checking, they turned out to be not so exceptional. Some applicants tell you about who and what they would like to be rather than who and what they really are. Don't assume that someone is even marginally competent, no matter how good he or she claims to be. Make the candi-date prove it through verified job performance. If he or she can't prove it, pass on to someone else.

My advice to companies is to make checking references the last hurdle in the employment process. In other words, go through the full evaluation process and then check references to be sure that what you have been led to believe about the person you have chosen for the job is, in fact, true. Some employers will get down to the last few candidates and then contact references to obtain information upon which to base a final selection decision. I don't recommend this as an effective way to use reference checking because it places too much emphasis on what the references have to say, and even more important, it strains the whole system through the heavy workload it creates. Checking out a large number of final candidates is also dangerous because those who are rejected may think it was caused by their references not speaking well of them, which may not be the case at all.

Checking the background of job candidates has never been more important. On the other hand, owing to reorganizations and downsizing, most companies and the people who do the employment screening have less time than ever to devote to the task. They are already overworked, and consequently this function often gets neglected. We are into a new era that requires new thinking and actions to get us back on track.

Avoiding the Problem Altogether

You can avoid hiring totally unknown people by being your own recruiter. There is nothing that prevents an organization from going out on its own to recruit proven, top performers whom it knows about. Most line or staff managers belong to associations or have some contact with other people in their specialty or career field. They have met or at least heard about individuals with excellent reputations. If you're looking for a state tax supervisor, for example, think of those with a top standing in this field. Call these people and let them know you have a position opening. If they are interested, have them come in or at least ask them to think about it and to call you back if they would like to pursue the opportunity.

Any employment specialist worth his salt will always ask the manager with an opening if he or she knows of anyone in particular who would fit in the job. Then you can start your search with these candidates. If you turn an opening over to an outside recruiting firm, it will often ask if there are any individuals you would really like to interview. It will then contact those persons and, if possible, feed them back to you. Why not avoid the expense and do it yourself? If it bothers you to make this contact as a representative of your company, hire someone to do it at a fraction of what you would have to pay to have these people eventually sent to you as a result of an expensive outside search effort.

Because of the difficulty of trying to screen job candidates today, a rapidly growing trend among organizations is to use temporary employees who can be cut loose if they aren't suitable or are not working out well on the job. A company can then hire permanent employees from this pool of people, after observing them over a period of time. The temp-to-hire program allows you to evaluate candidates on a trial basis before hiring them. However, there is a downside to using these people. The cost per hour for their services can be much higher than what you would pay if they were on your payroll.

If you are looking for a job and hear that a certain company that you would like to work for has an opening, contact that company and let the people there know of your interest before they have to start an expensive and time-consuming recruiting effort. You may find that you have practically clear sailing into the job. Send them a list of ten ways in which you can help the company meet its goals. Why wait for the opening to appear in the newspaper, when you then become just one of the many unknown respondents with whom a company has to deal?

The experience of most employers is that the best candidates come through referrals from employees, customers, professional networks, trade organizations, and even schools and churches. Use all the resources available to you. Paying employees a fee for referrals who are hired and stay for three months, six months, or a year is often a bargain in the recruiting process.

A little initiative by both the employer and the candidate can go a long way toward helping to solve the dilemma of the unknown applicant who has to be carefully screened and checked out in order to avoid unexpected future surprises after he or she starts work.

Part I Summary

The growing problem of dishonesty is a major business concern today. In Part I you found that:

▶ We live in a world where many people routinely lie and cheat and suffer no consequences for their behavior, setting a terrible example for all to follow.

▶ If you don't check out what people tell you, many questionable individuals will take advantage of the situation and gain access to jobs they are not qualified to hold.

▶ Eventually, even honest people will resort to falsification in order to keep up with the dishonest ones who are getting by on false pretenses.

▶ All these factors come into play, causing increasing dishonesty in the job market today. Therefore, now more than ever, you need to be diligent and thoroughly check out what you are told by job applicants.

Part II

Employment—A Legal Nightmare for Employers, and a Gold Mine for Lawyers

4

What's Legal and What's Not

Different hiring professionals look at legal issues in two different ways. Some clearly want to check applicants' backgrounds to ensure that everything is all right, and they want to be sure they are doing it legally. Another group wants to learn about and be conversant with the legal reasons why it is not advisable to check up on people, because deep down they just don't want to do it. They become part of the problem, instead of part of the solution.

I warn you in advance that those in the first group will be very pleased with this discussion, whereas the second group will be sorely disappointed. In this chapter, I am going to take a look at what legally can be done, not at what can't be done, in getting information about a job candidate's past actions and performance.

Basic Civil Rights

Let's first look at this matter from a historical perspective. There was a time, not long ago, when the "best jobs" were filled primarily by white men. Then, as a result of long overdue governmental and societal pressures, employers were forced to interview and consider women and minority group members for all job openings. To try to end discrimination in employment, federal and state governments passed laws and regulations to ensure that everyone would be treated equally and fairly when seeking jobs.

Let's look at it this way. We all know we have to "jump hurdles" to get a new job with a company; this is commonly referred to as going through the employment process. Now, if a white male has three hurdles; a white female, four hurdles; a minority female, five hurdles, and a minority male, six hurdles, this would be fair—at least not for those with the extra hurdles. Everyone should be subject to the same terms and rules when being considered for employment. That's just being fair! As an interviewer, you must be sure that you never violate a person's basic civil rights.

Asking the Right Questions

Many hours and dollars have been spent trying to train hiring officials as to what questions they can legally ask of job applicants and their references. From my experience, this training is usually presented in a very legalistic and complicated manner that ends up confusing those doing the hiring; in the end, it just makes them more frightened and less effective at checking out job candidates. You can boil it all down to two basic rules that will keep you out of trouble 99 and 44/100 percent of the time.

1. Ask the same questions. Don't use different questions for different groups (women, minority members, the handicapped).
2. Ask only job-related questions. Do not ask

for personal information. Play it safe. Stay with questions that have to do with education, training, work history, and job-related skills.

Using a typical situation, let's look at what is meant by asking all applicants the same questions. Suppose you are interviewing a mother of two young children for a secretarial position. Can you ask her how she is going to take care of these children while she is working? No, because you wouldn't ask a man this question, and besides, it is not related to her ability to perform her work. You can, however, define the job conditions for her, explaining that she may periodically have to work overtime on short notice, or that she will be expected to work about one Saturday per month. Then, with this background, you can ask her if your job fits and meets her personal and family needs. Exactly what her child care arrangements are is none of your concern.

Or, let's take the case of a young minority factory applicant who, as you have noticed from your office window, drives an old, dilapidated automobile. Can you ask him during the employment interview if his car will be able to get him to and from work? Again, the answer is no, because you wouldn't ask the same question of another applicant (who may be driving his father's new car), and the question is not related to his ability to do the job. Again, however, you can define the hours and conditions of work, which, let's say, are 7:00 A.M. to 4:00 P.M., with the necessity for working overtime as needed. You might also explain that the local bus, which goes by the plant, operates only from 6:00 A.M. to 6:00 P.M. With this background, you can then ask the young man if he will be able to get to work on time and to get home at the end of his shift. How he will do this is his problem and not yours.

The point is that you cannot create "extra hurdles" for some candidates, beyond those that are already laid out for other applicants. Your questions must be related to the job, which, when you really stop to think about it, is the only fair way to treat job applicants.

Now that you have this background, look at Exhibit 4-1, which specifies what you can and cannot ask in certain areas. Also, these interpretations on legal questions will apply to what you can ask when checking references, as you will see later in Chapter 12.

Preventing Employment Discrimination

There is a very fundamental concept in employment that must be honored. The nature of the questions you ask cannot reduce the chances of being hired of minorities, women, or other specified groups. You must be able to show that the responses to any questions asked are not used to eliminate any member of a protected class from consideration. In other words, if the answer you get becomes a factor in your decision, and it will eliminate a member of any single group, you had better be sure it does not get into a possible discrimination area. You would do better to avoid asking about or discussing anything—even if it's brought up by the candidate—that involves a person's sex, race, color, religion, national origin, age, or physical disability.

Exhibit 4-1. Legal inquiries before hiring.

Under federal law there cannot be job discrimination based on sex, race, color, religion, national origin, age, or physical disability. Consequently, there are questions you should not ask a prospective employee because they may be discriminatory.

Item	You Can Ask	You Cannot Ask About
Age	Whether candidate is above minimum or maximum age	Age, birth date, birth certificate, high school graduation date
Criminal Record	About a conviction record if it relates to ability to do the job	Arrest record
Credit Rating	Anything that directly relates to the job	Anything that does not relate to ability to do the job
Disabilities	Anything that has been proven to relate to ability to do the job	Anything that has not been proven to relate to ability to do the job
Work Schedule	About willingness to work required work schedule	Willingness to work any particular religious holiday
Marital/Family Status	Nothing	Anything
Military Record	About type of experience related to the job	Military service in any other country
National Origin	Whether candidate can legally work in the United States	Anything else
Race, Religion, Sex	Nothing	Anything

Caution: Be sure your employment policy is based on completely consistent company practices for investigating backgrounds and for making decisions not to hire. Candidates who feel they were rejected for reasons other than their qualifications may sue on grounds of discrimination. And companies that can't prove they subject every candidate to the same background investigation and the same hiring standards won't find it easy to defend themselves against such charges of discriminatory hiring practices.

These are hazy distinctions, I grant you, but the point to keep in mind is that if you're ever called upon to defend yourself against the charge that a certain question or series of questions reduced the chances of hiring a minority or female candidate, you will have to prove that the answer given was not used as a basis for your hiring decision. To repeat, questions must be job-related.

Interview Small Talk

One of the biggest problems in the interview process is the occasional innocent question that has absolutely nothing to do with the job opening or that asks for information the employer will not use in making a hiring decision. Many times such questions are raised in the small talk at the beginning of the interview, for example: "Do you have any kids?" or "What church do you attend?" Are these questions in and of themselves illegal? No, but if you were to use the responses to them as a reason for your employment decision, then they could be illegal.

Even if you haven't used questions like these to make your decision, merely having asked them raises the possibility in the applicant's mind that the responses may have been a factor in this final decision. Litigation could well be the result of such a misconception. You should, therefore, ask job-related questions only.

What do you do when the candidate, in an attempt to make conversation or in answering your questions, freely throws out more personal information to you? Most hiring experts advise you to quickly change the subject. I suppose this is probably good advice, but in real life, is that the way it's always done?

I discussed this subject with a hiring manager from a company known for its high standards and low turnover. He said that if somebody wants to "run their mouth," he let's them do so and does not try to stop or limit such talk. He explained that if you listen you may find out things about someone that will help you make your hiring decision. He noted that what is said between two people in private is really impossible to challenge or verify later on. In his view, regardless of what the legal experts say, there is a reality about all this that we shouldn't ignore or run from.

Of course, questions shouldn't be asked in the interview process if they elicit information about factors the employer is prohibited from considering in making employment decisions, such as marital status, national origin, or disability. If such information is elicited, the employer may then have a difficult task convincing a court or agency that the information wasn't, in fact, used in making the hiring decision.

The Need to Check an Applicant's Background

Many managers are unaware of the extent to which their organizations are accountable for the actions of their employees. Employers have been found liable for theft, sexual assault, robbery, and wrongful death owing to an employee's misconduct.

The employer can be held liable for an employee's unlawful acts when the employer does not reasonably investigate a potential employee's background and puts the employee in a position to commit crimes, thus exposing others to the risk of harm or injury from that employee.

As a rule, employers may be found liable if:

▶ The injury or harm is foreseeable.
▶ Hiring or retaining the employee puts him or her in a position to commit the act, even though the act is beyond his or her job responsibilities.
▶ The employer knew or should have known, based on a reasonable investigation, that the employee was not suitable for the duties of the position.

Employers are not always exposed to liability just because they fail to check an applicant's background. Liability results only when the inadequate screening effort is logically connected with the wrongful act.

The federal government and many states have laws requiring applicants in certain fields to undergo a background check before they are hired. Many states, for example, require background checks before qualifying attorneys, private investigators, law enforcement officials, and child care providers.

So how much screening is enough to avoid liability? The amount of screening must be proportionate to the degree of risk presented by the job to be filled. The focus must be on the position to be filled, not on the applicant.

Does It Really Happen?

Here are some actual stories of people who were not what their employers thought they would be.

A court found a security company liable when one of its guards (with a criminal record for violence) struck a woman in the building he was guarding because she questioned his authority. The company hired the guard and put him on the job before receiving a criminal background report.

In finding the security company liable, the court stated that it was the company's responsibility to check into the guard's background prior to putting him on the job. The court went on to say that a reasonably adequate investigation would have determined that the guard was unfit for this job. Had the security company performed a timely investigation, it probably would not have hired the guard.

A manufacturer fired an employee when it was discovered that he was using drugs on the job. After he was terminated, the employee was hired by another company in the same town, where he was eventually caught stealing company property and using drugs. The police were called in and the employee was arrested.

Neither company had checked his record before hiring him. Had they done so, both would have found a history of drug-related discharges.

A woman who posed as a physician was arrested by state investigators at the clinic where she worked. She was charged with two felony counts of using fraudulent records to obtain employment as a physician and misdemeanor counts of practicing medicine without a license and unlawfully representing herself as a doctor, according to the State Medical Board.

She obtained her job in the clinic with the help of a false physician's identification card and a false document from the Federal Drug Enforcement Agency authorizing her to dispense medication. She had also faked documents indicating that she had received medical training at universities in Mexico, California, and Colorado. A more thorough review of her background would most likely have revealed that she was operating under false pretenses.

Authorization and Release

Employers should include in their job application forms, usually at the end, a clear statement that: (1) a background check will be performed on every person the company is considering hiring; and (2) the applicant authorizes such a check and releases the company from all liability for performing the investigation. By signing this authorization, the applicant acknowledges that he has read the release and consents to a background check that will include reference checks with prior employers, and may also cover criminal, worker's compensation, credit, and driving records.

5

Legal Doublespeak

Employers are between a rock and a hard place. Attorneys giving advice on what to tell someone who contacts them about a past employee will advise employers not to give out any information—except name, rank, and serial number. In other words, provide only dates of employment and job title, and perhaps verify salary level if the caller already knows it. They say it is dangerous to go beyond these facts because doing so could lead to a lawsuit by a dissatisfied past employee.

The very same attorneys will then tell you to get all the information you can about a prospective employee, because employer liability for bad hiring decisions is on the rise. Since the early 1980s, more courts have held companies legally responsible for the actions of their employees, and have gone so far as to point out that a company was actually negligent in the way it went about hiring an individual. Damage awards in such cases can be substantial.

This amounts to legal doublespeak. Don't tell anyone anything when contacted, but expect them to tell you everything when you contact them. In my own reference checking business, I have been amazed at how often client companies ask me to get all the background data and information about a prospective employee that I can lay my hands on; yet, when I contact these same companies to get information for someone else,

they tell me that company policy prohibits them
from giving any information to anyone. Everyone
from top to bottom seems thoroughly confused
by this critical legal issue.

I once asked a prominent attorney why his
fellow members of the legal profession would not
advise their client companies to start releasing information on past employees in order to balance
out the problem. He replied that, in his opinion,
lawyers just don't want to admit they've been
wrong. Another attorney explained to me that
corporate "blackout" policies probably reflect the
influence of ultraconservative legal departments.

I can personally tell you that this business of
speaking out of both sides of the mouth doesn't
play well anymore. Increasingly, I hear attorneys
challenged by audience members during presen-
tations they are giving on employment law. Hiring officials ask how it is that they can be
instructed to get all the information they can
when considering someone for employment
when the very people they are to get it from are
told not to give it to them. One person in the audience compared this situation to a doctor writing a
prescription for you, then telling every druggist
in town not to sell you the medicine.

The whole game has become very confusing
to everyone, especially those charged with getting
or giving out information on employees. They are
damned if they do and damned if they don't. An
employer is held liable for disclosing too much
information or too little information, or for failing
to get enough information about the termination
of an employee. Many are quite confused and
even upset over this conflicting legal advice.
There is a school of thought that the legal entan-

glements we continually create and our inability to deal realistically with them is a serious problem in this country. Employment law may just be a prime example of this.

Unfortunately, the traditional legal advice has helped to create the current problems in this area: "Get all the information you can, but don't give out any." Not only is this poor legal advice, it's terrible management advice. It has led to paranoia in the hiring process and to lies on applications and résumés. Some attorneys who work in this field, however, have been offering a different approach, as we shall see. In the meantime, everyone is confused on the subject, and even the attorneys are fighting among themselves.

As a practical matter, what goes around comes around, and an employer who gives only minimal information is likely to meet similar roadblocks when the company's human resources officials seek references.

As a policy matter, too, more management lawyers are questioning the wisdom of an approach that allows bad employees to pass from employer to employer and punishes good employees who deserve the benefit of a positive referral.

Companies withholding information have in effect rewarded the poor performer and penalized the good one by not revealing pertinent information about someone's past job performance. That's hardly sensible, much less fair. They literally have turned the whole employment game upside down so that the bad guys are winning and the good guys are losing.

In New Zealand there is a vine that is especially troublesome. It has small hooks that stick to your clothing, and the more you struggle to free yourself, the more entangled you become. The New Zealanders, who have a sense of humor about such things, call this annoying fact of life on the North Island the "lawyer vine." Has the employment area become our "lawyer vine"?

The Real Problem In Employment

In my view, lawyers have effectively crippled the nation's hiring efforts and encouraged lying, cover-ups, and failure by telling companies not to talk with each other about past employees.

There are several reasons why I make these claims:

▶ *Lying:* Knowing that their work history probably won't be checked, many candidates lie and get away with it, which is causing even honest applicants to cheat to stay in the running. For example, an applicant for a well-paying position as a systems analyst with a large company told me, "I'm going to say whatever it takes to get the job because it won't be checked out," explaining that he just wanted to beat out his competition for the position.

▶ *Cover-ups:* Protecting poor performers and penalizing those with good records is hardly a fair way to reward good service. One distraught woman called me saying, "I worked hard for my last employer and was always rated an outstanding employee until I lost my job due to severe downsizing in the company. Now they won't talk to anyone about me, which makes it sound like I was a poor employee."

▶ *Failure:* Being told to check out the people you hire when everyone else has been told not to provide such information means you are literally setting yourself up to fail. Most hiring officials readily admit that they won't exchange information with each other because their attorneys have instructed them not to. I believe attorneys rate a D minus for the way they have guided the American employment scene. It is my hope that this book will help to straighten out the mess they have created.

The Cost of Running Scared

A certain amount of legal expense should be considered as part of the normal cost of doing business. Ironically, many companies today are spending more to prevent lawsuits related to employment practices than it would cost them to defend against such suits if they were brought.

Actually, the direct cost of defending oneself in such lawsuits is normally quite small because few actions result in suits. The threat of litigation, more than actual lawsuits themselves, is causing companies to behave in ways that drive up hiring costs and also affect their very ability to hire.

One of the possible hidden costs to companies is the expense of hiring poor performers rather than passing over them. In addition, some companies, as part of their defensive strategy, may be providing more overtime pay to a reduced work force or using easy-to-terminate but expensive temporary workers instead of hiring full-time employees. These indirect costs can well exceed the cost of defending themselves against legal actions.

Companies are behaving as if the odds of being sued are much higher than they actually are. Whereas employers once felt they had considerable leeway in choosing their employees, they have now gone too far in the other direction. There is no question that legal and regulatory considerations cannot be ignored, but interpretations of employment law in each state have been both broad and narrow, and vary greatly from state to state and even from case to case.

The legal picture is somewhat different in the employment setting. First, it is very difficult for applicants to determine why they were turned down for a job. Second, the burden of proving that statements by a company representative about a past or current employee were false or that they were made carelessly, recklessly, or maliciously are very difficult burdens for the plaintiff to meet.

Indeed, running scared is probably the least effective (and most costly) way to handle employment problems. The strategies and techniques suggested in this book are safer and less expensive than the defensive actions you may be taking. Simply reducing your legal exposure is not necessarily the best way to go about hiring or to get the work force you need.

6

New Directions in Employment Screening

The proper exchange of employment information is a legal necessity. I talk about hiring issues with many employers, and I also talk with leading attorneys whose practices include labor and employment law. The attorneys emphasize the following points:

- ▶ Learn as much as you can about a person before you extend a job offer.
- ▶ Don't hire if you're unsure about a candidate's past activities and accomplishments.

The increase in workplace violence and negligent hiring lawsuits provides good business and legal justification for employers to perform background checks on all potential employees.

Performing a background check on a job applicant minimizes the employer's exposure. Conversely, if an employee later harms a customer or another employee and no pre-employment investigation was done, exposure can be significant. The employer may face liability for negligent hiring. Clearly, pre-employment screening is a business necessity in today's environment.

Consequently, it is time for companies to get rid of old ideas and start exercising their right to check out job candidates thoroughly. The pendulum is swinging back—from winging it on soft information to digging it out with due diligence.

Negligent Hiring

Attorneys today are very concerned about negligent hiring, which is the failure to exercise reasonable care and judgment when filling a position. It is the employer's responsibility to find out the truth about a potential employee. If the employer chooses to hire an individual without checking his or her background, then the employer must be willing to accept the risk that something might go wrong when that person goes to work. Often, this is a no-win situation. For example, if a taxi service hires a driver who assaults a passenger, a lawsuit may result from the driver's conduct. The company may have adequate legal defense but chooses to back down to avoid notoriety or simply to spare itself the costs of protracted litigation.

Negligent hiring claims have proliferated over the last several years and often arise when an employee causes violence in the workplace. Like product liability claims (which argue that, by virtue of having a product on the market, a manufacturer is responsible for harm to the public arising from the use of that product), negligent hiring claims argue that, by virtue of having someone on the payroll, an employer is responsible for harm to the public caused by that employee. Like all negligence claims, however, negligent hiring typically hinges on whether or not an employer took reasonable precautions to prevent the incident.

As I explain in my seminars on employment screening, negligent hiring is a consideration, although, frankly, I have run across very few individuals or companies that got into trouble for something they did (or didn't do) during the hiring process. However, there may be negligence if new employees do not work out as expected and yet are retained by the company. Someone hired these mistakes in the first place, meaning that someone or a number of people in the company did not do their jobs well.

Negligent References

A new potential for liability is that courts may be willing to hold employers liable for negligent references. In other words, a previous employer may know that someone has traits that make him or her a menace to others, but fail to disclose the information to a prospective employer.

Each situation has its own set of circumstances. But companies can no longer assume that they are safe so long as they say nothing. Failure to state why an employee was dismissed, even if defamatory, may carry as much risk as candidly stating the facts. Most employers have adopted the most conservative position possible, limiting the information they provide to employees' job titles and dates of employment. In doing so, they prevent other employers from gathering requisite information about employees' job histories and work performance—key data in making hiring decisions, data they themselves seek when hiring their own employees.

An old, hard-nosed production manager I know has a policy that he openly announces to his employees: If he is ever contacted about them after they leave the company, he will be very frank about their job performance. If they were good he will say so; if they were bad he will tell that to anyone who contacts him. He reminds his workers not to let him down or to "dog it" just because they think they're leaving the company and it won't matter anyway. I have heard him tell a marginal worker, "I will go out of my way to tell anyone who needs to know that you were a sorry employee when you worked for me." Knowing that he won't hesitate to relay that opinion to others makes his employees stop and think about whether they want to be described as poor workers. And, as far as I can tell, it has been an effective motivational tool for him. Some people might question the legality and fairness of this technique, but what could be more fair to everyone concerned than good old-fashioned truthfulness? We used to call it "telling it like it is."

If nondisclosure policies continue, they will cause more lawsuits than they prevent. Defamation and invasion of privacy claims will disappear, but negligent hiring and retention suits will replace them. Employers should examine their policies as to the release of employee information and take advantage of the "qualified privilege" doctrine that states that they can release information without fear of being sued if they do it properly. It's time to turn around the trend that is causing negligent hiring lawsuits.

Should You Give References?

Information about job candidates is exchanged informally all the time. Friends talk to friends; employees of one company talk to employees of another company; managers talk to other managers in their specialty; and certainly executives talk to other executives and even sit on the same boards of directors with them. Job seekers often list current members of a company as personal references, which means that they want these people to talk freely with potential employers. The point is simply that job-related information is constantly exchanged in the everyday world—regardless of what attorneys may advise.

In fact, many companies today are sitting down with their attorneys in an effort to update their policies and practices on checking references, to make them more realistic and practical. And as a matter of note, I have never had an attorney I contacted (as a reference for a person he or she knew) who did not fully cooperate with me and provide complete information about the applicant. And this is based on hundreds of such contacts.

More and more attorneys now advise employers to release information with caution. One attorney I spoke with commented, "We are going to have to start being more cooperative [when] giving each other information—particularly if you think you are dealing with someone who might harm someone else." Another attorney told me, "Companies can get into trouble only if managers discuss personal issues or release age or other data subject to discrimination."

One employer I know will, as matter of policy, actually read over the phone the last performance review of a former employee. I think this is a stroke of genius, because it means that a performance evaluation, which we know determines an employee's future in the company, now has an important bearing when the person is making a job change. Knowing this, a person would be foolish to let his performance slip because this poor performance record will be made known to anyone with a legitimate need to know about it. Not giving out past performance information encourages mediocrity in that it removes a major incentive for trying to maintain a good work record.

By the way, a large number of employers, as a matter of practice, give a copy of the performance review to the employee being rated. When you are hiring, why not ask to see the applicant's last two or three performance reviews? Or, if contacted for information about a past employee, why not suggest that the prospective employer ask to see the candidate's copy of past performance reviews given by your company? This is information that is already developed and doesn't put any reference on the spot about the candidate. Of course, to do this, you need to be confident that your company has strong and consistent performance evaluation procedures that you are willing to stand behind.

Another suggestion in regard to giving reference information is to have, as part of the separation process, a form that terminated employees can sign to indicate whether they want reference data to be given out after they leave the company. If they allow their employment record to be discussed, do it. If they don't, explain that fact to the prospective employer and suggest that the employer review the matter with the candidate to determine why he or she did not authorize such information to be exchanged. Exhibit 6-1 is a sample Approval to Release Employment Information form.

The Law and Good Business

The law is very much on the side of employers. Employers have a right to discuss their employees with others who have a common interest in them. It's a fundamental legal principle that neither true statements nor statements of opinion can be defamatory, no matter how hurtful they are. Indeed, employers are liable for defamation only if they knowingly or recklessly spread *false* information.

The bottom line is that it is not illegal to get or to give references. The decision to do one or both should be based on all the factors that influence any normal business decision, such as whether an effort is worth the expected return. Various companies weigh these factors and come to different conclusions. For example, many companies have decided to discontinue company picnics because of the legal and financial danger that such events can create. They looked at the problems that could develop from too much drinking, sports injuries, or whatever else might happen at such unstructured events, and decided they were just no longer worth the effort. Yet other companies have looked at the same factors and decided that they can live with them. The point is that, although there are legal factors to consider, having a company picnic is certainly not illegal.

Exhibit 6-1. Approval to release employment information form.

When the human resources department receives a request from a prospective employer for information about a former employee, we furnish only limited information concerning:

      (a)   dates of employment;
      (b)   last job title or classification, and
            last applicable wage rate/salary.

We do not discuss orally, or in writing, the individual's work performance, reason for leaving, or any other information that we consider to be confidential. This confidential information is divulged only when the past employee has specifically directed us to do so.

Therefore, we would be willing to furnish such additional information if you sign the form below and return it to us. If you do not want to do this, we will advise the prospective employer that, although we can provide such information, you have not authorized us to do so. In either event, this form must be signed and sent to:

Human Resources Manager
The ABC Company
1115 Any Street
Cincinnati, OH 12345

Print Your Name Here: _____
(Sign one space below)

I hereby authorize the ABC Company to release confidential information concerning my employment record to prospective employers upon their legitimate request for same. I acknowledge that some information divulged may be negative or positive with respect to my performance and agree that I release The ABC Company, its agents, and employees from any and all liability for furnishing such information upon proper request.

_____
(Signature)   (Date)

I do not authorize The ABC Company to reveal information about my past employment record to anyone, including a prospective employer.

_____
(Signature)   (Date)

Employment screening should involve a careful assessment of the prospective employee's résumé or application as well as contact with previous employers and personal references.

In some situations, an employer is well advised to research an applicant's past criminal record. Such a search is not necessary in all cases, as long as the employer makes an adequate inquiry into the prospective employee's general and job-specific fitness. A criminal record search, however, is particularly appropriate when an applicant's position involves safety, protection of property, or any risk of harm to co-workers or customers.

State Protection for Employers

Many states have now enacted legislation to protect employers from civil liabilities when providing good faith references for former employees. In recent years, twenty-two states have passed laws providing employers who release truthful information with varying degrees of protection from suits alleging defamation and other claims. The laws, intended to make the workplace safer and more efficient, are prompting companies to reevaluate their policies. Similar bills are pending in other states.

The states that have already passed such laws are Arizona, California, Colorado, Florida, Georgia, Idaho, Illinois, Indiana, Kansas, Louisiana, Maine, Michigan, New Mexico, Ohio, Oklahoma, Oregon, South Carolina, South Dakota, Tennessee, Utah, Wisconsin, and Wyoming.

In the states that have passed legislation,

many employers are reluctant to use the laws. A lot of it has to do with corporate policies. Some employers don't seem to trust the law and aren't willing to change their corporate policies. They seem confused as to how they can use the law to improve their hiring process. The observation was made by one state legislator that in many ways the easy part was passing the legislation and that educating employers and getting them to change their ways is the greater challenge.

I certainly suggest that if you are in a state that has passed new reference checking laws, it behooves you to understand the scope and advantages of the law.

Who's Running HR? The Attorneys?

The decision to release information should be based on sound business and commonsense considerations. Human resources professionals need to be willing to make these decisions rather than simply to cite company policy in the erroneous belief that in this way they've minimized their company's risk. After all, isn't that what professionals in any field are paid to do?

With so many issues affecting hiring, one would think that human resources officials would be in the driver's seat. But, far too often, we find these professionals deferring to attorneys when it comes to tough employment policy decisions.

When a proposed course of action is legal and in compliance with applicable regulations, why delay or question its implementation? Do you need an attorney's opinion if you know your action is sound and legal?

I know HR managers who take the lead (and risk) by managing and directing their functional area. These professionals welcome challenge and want to be on the cutting edge rather than waiting to be told what to do. They enjoy being innovative and doing the right thing, unlike those HR custodians who do only what they are told to do by counsel.

There is no question that companies need guidance on how to handle complex human resources issues. But playing it safe—relying on legal counsel on an almost daily basis—raises the legitimate question: What is HR's value to the organization? I hope HR executives heed this wake-up call. It could well save the day for them.

Simplified Guidelines

In most states, companies have a legal right—and some courts say even a moral obligation—to provide prospective employers with an honest and candid appraisal of their former employees. The law may be summarized by the equation given in Exhibit 6-2.

That is, when a prospective employer is seeking information needed to make an informed and rational hiring decision, and the former employer relates his former employee's work history in a factual manner without making statements that are known falsehoods, then the law protects the communication from a successful legal action by the former employee. If an employer stays within the boundaries of "qualified privilege," a fear of lawsuits is not justified under current law.

When it comes to answering requests for job

Exhibit 6-2. The factors making up qualified privilege.

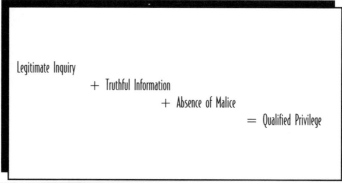

Legitimate Inquiry
    + Truthful Information
        + Absence of Malice
            = Qualified Privilege

references, you and your staff don't have to clam up. Instead, you can cooperate and at the same time protect yourself in two ways. First, tell the truth. Provide an honest, specific evaluation of a former employee's work and abilities. Second, communicate only with someone who has a need to know. In legal lingo, most states allow an employer who is acting in good faith a "qualified privilege" to say things that would otherwise be considered defamatory. But you can lose this protection by providing more information than a prospective employer needs to satisfy its legitimate business interests or by communicating information to people who don't need to know at all.

You will also lose the privilege's protection if a former employee can prove that you acted maliciously and intended harm or that you recklessly provided false or inaccurate information.

Exhibits 6-3 and 6-4 cover the legal interpretations regarding getting and giving references and the basic rules to follow when giving references. They provide a capsulized view of the whole legal issue.

Exhibit 6-3. Legal interpretations relevant to hiring and giving references.

Negligent hiring—a claim that the employer did not go far enough in checking references and hired someone who later caused injury to a co-worker or customer. The basis for damages is that the employer should have conducted a more thorough background check that would have revealed the person's likelihood of injuring someone while on the job.

A major car rental company hired a car-washer who had a prison record as a rapist. The employee raped a secretary in the office during work hours. The secretary was awarded $750,000 in damages, because the company had not done a background check on the employee. The court ruled that the employer had a duty to the other employees to investigate applicants before they are hired.

Defamation—an allegation by a plaintiff that his or her reputation was damaged as the result of an employer's disclosure of false information to third persons, or the giving of a bad reference to someone who was not privileged to receive the information.

Defamation involves a false or defamatory statement resulting in damage to the employee's reputation. Defamation can take two forms.

1. *slander,* in cases where an alleged defamatory statement is spoken, for example, a supervisor telling a co-worker that someone was fired for stealing.
2. *libel,* in cases of written statements, such as a termination notice that says an employee was fired for sexual harassment.

Invasion of privacy—a suit alleging that management disclosed information that should have been kept secret.

The type of invasion of privacy claim that is most often found in the employment setting involves public disclosure of private facts. Even though the private facts may be true, the employer is held liable for their disclosure simply because they are private facts.

Exhibit 6-4. Giving references legally.

Most courts' rulings on reference checking have said that a former employer can give out information on a past employee that is pertinent to making a hiring decision, so long as the information is true or reasonably believed to be so. Basically, the courts in all states have held that employers, both former and prospective, have a "qualified privilege" to discuss an employee's past performance. When the information is given to someone with a clear need to receive it, discussion of an employee's past performance, good or bad, is permissible by law.

The law favors the release of background information among employers. This privilege is founded on a policy of promoting reliable business judgments in hiring, based on all the knowledge available in the business community. Thus, when a company releases background information that enables a potential employer to make a better hiring decision, as long as the statements are true, there is no liability for libel or slander because such statements were made in furtherance of this important social policy.

To comply with equal employment opportunity considerations and rulings, all questions asked and answers given must be job-related, indicative of the individual's ability to perform the job and of his or her personality characteristics as they relate to how that person gets along with others in the work setting.

Legal Guidelines

☑ *Procedure:*

1. Policy—Provide the same type of information for employees at all levels.
2. Legitimate—Communicate only with someone who has a need to know the information, normally a personnel officer or the supervisor to whom the employees will report on the new job.
3. Document—Keep a written log of the date information was communicated and the person spoken with.
4. Consent—The new employer must have written consent from the job candidate to contact references, normally part of signing off the employment application.

☑ *Information:*

5. Truthful—The information given must be true to the best of your knowledge and there must be no intent to ruin the person's reputation. It is best if your facts can be supported by proper documentation.
6. Job-related—Limit the information you provide to job-related data only.
7. Not malicious—Never give unnecessary and malicious information just to provide a better understanding of the past employee (or to harm the individual).
8. Don't volunteer—Answer only the actual inquiry without giving an opinion or making a conjecture.

(To win a lawsuit, the candidate would have to prove that 5 through 8, above, were violated and that there was resulting damage and financial loss.)

This information is general in nature; it does not take into account specific state laws or regulations, and is not meant to replace the advice of a qualified attorney in the area of employment law.

Part II Summary

Summarizing the legal issues in checking out applicants is not that difficult. In Part II of this book you have learned that:

▶ The law does not say that you cannot check the backgrounds of those individuals you are thinking of hiring.

▶ There is a very slight danger that releasing information about a past employee could result in a lawsuit, but unless someone's basic rights have been violated, there is little chance that the suit will be successful.

▶ Anything you do in business can result in a legal problem; in fact, you wouldn't be in business if you were afraid of such complications.

▶ The attorneys who advise employers on hiring people are somewhat isolated from the daily problems of the workplace and do not have to suffer the consequences of their advice.

▶ The choice to check the references of prospective employees is simply another business decision you have to make.

▶ These points make it clear that the decision not to check references or not to give reference information to other employers is really a matter of choosing not to spend the necessary time and effort to do it.

Part III

Keeping the
Applicant Honest

7

Making Sure People Are Honest With You

Honesty is the best policy. But how do you convince job applicants of this? There apparently is something of a trend in this country toward being a "nice interviewer." Many managers, for example, don't want to offend or ruffle a candidate, so they ask easy and sometimes pointless questions rather than the difficult or meaningful ones that might elicit the applicant's deepest thoughts, feelings, and abilities.

The trouble is that nice people are sitting ducks for all the dishonest applicants crowding the job market today. We know there are individuals who will say anything so long as it helps them to get the job they want. When you evaluate someone for employment, your role is not to make a new friend but to be sure your company is hiring the right person. You don't have to be a tough guy to do this; in fact, being tough doesn't guarantee that you won't get fooled. What best protects you from being taken advantage of is being completely in control of the hiring process.

What I advocate in handling and screening employees is a style midway between being nice and tough. That is, treat candidates fairly and firmly right down to the words, phrases, and mannerisms you use. You need to take control from the start and stay in control throughout the hiring process. In the coming pages, I will show you how to do just that. For some of you it may require being a little more tough-minded than you have been. But if you do what I recommend, it will become quite easy to stay in charge all the way through the hiring process. Success comes from being in complete control of the situation.

Listening Aggressively

If you listen to and observe people carefully, they will tell you almost everything you want or need to know in order to make enlightened decisions. Even though people are often inconsistent, they do reveal themselves in time. But first you have to know how to listen.

When interviewing someone or checking references, it is critical to hear what is really being said. Most interviewers literally talk their way out of the information being supplied by concentrating their attention on what they are saying rather than on listening to what the interviewee is saying.

Instead of mentally rehearsing the next point on your agenda or the next question you wish to ask, listen and respond spontaneously. Probe, question, and follow up until you are fully satisfied with the answers you have been given and feel reasonably confident that what you have heard is true. In other words, never stop questioning until you have the information you seek.

Not only must you pay attention to *what* is being said; you must also listen to *how* it's said. By this I mean voice expression, underlying intent, or any hidden clues. I suggest you stop a minute and think of an important conversation you have had recently in which there were some underlying or special cues from the speaker that were critical to understanding the message being given. Examples of such cues include a clearing of the throat, a nervous laugh or a long pause. You probably picked up on such cues because they were so open and apparent. The secret is to be able to pick up on them when they are not so obvious—because they are there if you are alert enough to catch them.

One of the most potent ways to draw someone out in an interview is to pause or use silence. This technique usually makes the candidate uncomfortable, and he or she may then try to fill the void by providing more information. Most people, when they sense that another person is anxious, try to put him at his ease. Anxiety makes people uncomfortable. But if you can learn to allow the other person to be anxious, you may discover something important that you would otherwise have missed. Television interviewers and police officers use this technique with great effectiveness. Watch one of the well known and highly competent network TV hosts who will ask the guest a thoughtful question and then be totally quiet until it is answered. Try it. You'll be surprised at how most people simply can't stand the sudden quiet, and will rush to give you more details.

Finally, ask the applicant to name other people who can verify the information he or she has given you. This is absolutely critical for two reasons: (1) It tends to keep the respondent honest; and (2) it provides sources to contact who will validate what you have been told by the candidate and other references.

Ironically, most of the training for interviewers that I am familiar with emphasizes strong questioning techniques. Although the proper questions are of course vital to a good interview, too few interviewers know how to listen effectively and therefore never really hear what candidates are telling them.

Show the candidate you are listening. Look at his or her face. Lean a little toward the person. These seemingly small body language signals tell someone you are interested in what she has to say. Concentrate on the person's voice. As the person speaks, think about what she is saying. Above all, do not think about what you are going to say in response to the applicant's comments before she finishes speaking. If you are thinking about your next question, you cannot listen to what that person is saying at the moment. Besides, you can easily miss an important point. Even worse, you may miss a crucial clue about the candidate's honesty.

Speak less, listen more. If you'll allow them to, people will go to great lengths to explain why they think, feel, and act the way they do. And that information will help you make a better hiring decision.

Spotting Liars

Lying is nothing more than someone trying to make things the way he wants them to be rather than the way they really are.

There are two types of lies—*prepared lies* or

false statements planned ahead of time; and *spontaneous lies*, or false responses to an unexpected question. When people lie, their actions often give them away. People who tell prepared lies tend to give very brief answers, have tremors in their voice, or sound very rehearsed. People who tell spontaneous lies tend to give brief answers (most liars can't think of what to say quickly enough), make speaking errors such as "we was," or resort to meaningless phrases such as "you know" and "see what I mean." There are two primary ways to lie: to conceal and to falsify. In concealing, the liar withholds some information without actually saying anything untrue. In falsifying, the liar presents false information as if it were true.

Most liars don't want to go into a lot of detail. The best way to smoke them out, therefore, is to ask them to elaborate on what they have said. Since they hate to keep adding to their lies, they will usually show it by stumbling around or even completely freezing up. Not every little miscue means that someone is lying (people are nervous in interview situations, after all), but, if you suspect that someone is not being truthful, press harder to see if that is the case. If he or she isn't lying, no one will be the worse off, because both of you will gain more faith in each other as the result of the probing.

Of course, the best way to determine if someone is lying is through reference checking. These checks, done properly, will validate that what you have been told and led to believe about the applicant is, in fact, true and accurate. It just makes sense in today's world, where there is so much lying going on, to check out what people tell you.

8

A Proper Interview

The interview is the most appropriate place in which to identify references. I cannot tell you how many times I have gotten reference checking assignments in my private practice in which the client company had no idea or recommendation as to whom I should contact. The hiring managers have spent hours or even days interviewing and getting to know a prospective employee; yet they cannot name one significant person in the candidate's work life to talk to about the candidate. They have completely missed the opportunity to identify knowledgeable people who can either verify or refute the information furnished by the applicant.

Two Principles

As already explained, job seekers are well aware that what they say will probably never be checked out. Most employers leave it up to the candidate to list the people he or she would like contacted as references. The process is slanted toward the applicant, and this needs to be changed. So let's analyze the interview in its entirety, starting with two points that should be kept in mind if the interview is to be made a more meaningful exercise for the employer.

First Principle

Insist on honest answers from the job applicant. How do you do this? It's very simple: Make it very clear during the entire interview that nothing else will be tolerated. In other words, always keep your authority in view.

Our conscience works best when we know we're being watched. What happens when we're driving down the highway and all of a sudden we see a police officer up ahead? Almost by instinct, we lift our foot from the gas pedal, immediately glance at the speedometer, and probably put our foot on the brake. Or, what happens in a classroom when the teacher leaves the room? Usually, if it's a normal group of students, they start misbehaving.

The most feared words a candidate can hear are, "We are going to check your references." This means quite simply, "Be totally honest with us. Distorting your background won't fly here, and only the truth will work in getting the job." Many employers are going so far as to have applicants sign a statement as to the truthfulness of their answers to interview questions (see Exhibit 8-1 for an example). It will make even the most skillful imposter run for cover.

By the way, most attorneys advise that employers have the best protection from lawsuits if the applicant signs a clear release that allows the company to check his or her background and to contact references. If this is set forth in a separate document, rather than by the usual sign-off at the bottom of the employment application, it constitutes a much stronger legal document.

Exhibit 8-1. Employment statement signed by applicant prior to being hired.

Employment Statement
XYZ Company
123 Any Street
Atlanta, Georgia 12345

Date: _____

1. The background information supplied by an applicant for a position opening will be checked by XYZ Company or an outside reference checking service to ensure the accuracy of the data furnished and the past performance record of the candidate.

2. I authorize XYZ Company to make such investigations and inquiries as may be necessary in arriving at an employment decision. I hereby release employers, schools, or persons from all liability in responding to inquiries in connection with my application for employment.

3. I should not resign my current employment until I have received a formal offer of employment, in writing, signed by an XYZ Company Employment Representative.

4. XYZ Company retains the right to hire the person who appears to best fit its needs at this time. There will not be an explanation (unless specifically required by law) as to what factors went into this decision.

5. The answers given to XYZ Company representatives are true and complete to the best of my knowledge. In the event of employment, any significant misstatements or omissions later discovered in my background may be cause for my dismissal from XYZ Company.

_____
Candidate's Signature

_____
Print Full Name

_____
Social Security Number

Warn the applicant up front that all references will be checked. This reminder can go a long way toward making the individual see the need to be honest during the interview. Then, during the interview itself, insist on honest answers by making such statements as the following:

▶ Answer the question the way you think your references will.
▶ When we call your references, what do you think they will say?
▶ To whom should I talk to verify this point?

By giving a warning at the beginning, and during the interview, you have a tremendous influence on keeping the applicant honest—and it doesn't take any time to do it.

Second Principle

Identify and gather the names of meaningful references during the interview. How do you do this? Again, it's very simple: You need to identify the key players in the applicant's work life and write them down during the interview. In other words, choose your own references.

This is the only realistic way to do it. Otherwise you're letting the candidate furnish the references he chooses, which is not a very sensible approach. What you may end up with are names of the candidate's choosing, such as his minister, brother-in-law, or best friend. This is not to imply that these individuals will not be honest and reliable, but there are certainly more meaningful people with whom you can speak.

In my private reference checking practice, I can usually tell if the candidate whose references I am to check has a strong work record just by observing the references given. If the references are previous managers, company officials, or other important people in her work life, then the person is proud of her work history. Good candidates with a strong record of performance will have excellent references from former and present employers. If the names given are those of close friends, relatives, or others who have never really worked with the candidate, however, I suspect that she is hiding something. I'm usually right.

There is no reason not to identify at least six references during the interview. Get the names of the applicant's boss and the boss's boss, the names of two peers, and the names of two subordinates or other persons below the level of the candidate at every place the candidate has worked. I call it the $2+2+2=6$ (Exhibit 8-2). Obviously, you can do the same thing by adding $1+1+1=3$ or $3+3+3=9$. The point is that it's not that hard to develop key references for each one of the applicant's past employers.

Some companies instruct applicants to list on their employment application the names and telephone numbers of their previous supervisors. Exhibit 8-3 illustrates a separate form for this purpose. Just using this system will bring honesty to your hiring program. To see how this whole new checking system can come into play during your interviewing of a job candidate, study the sample interview forms shown in Exhibits 8-5 and 8-6 at the end of this chapter.

Exhibit 8-2. The $2 + 2 + 2 = 6$ formula for eliciting references.

Superiors:

_____

Name/Title   *(Boss's Boss)*

_____

Name/Title   *(Direct Supervisor)*

Peer: | Candidate: | *Peer:*

_____   _____   _____

Name/Title   Name   Name/Title
Inside Dept.   Outside Dept.

Subordinates:

_____

Name/Title   *(Direct Report)*

_____

Name/Title   *(Support Worker)*

Exhibit 8-3. Employment verification form.

Your application will not be given consideration if this is not completed.

Name: _____	S.S. No.: _____
Other Names Used: Dates: _____ _____ _____ _____ _____ _____	Under what name did you attend/graduate from high school/college? _____ Driver's License No. State (If driving is required on the job) _____ ____

Have you ever been convicted of a felony? ☐ Yes ☐ No
(If yes, answer a & b.)
a) Location (city, county, state): _____ Date _____
b) Nature of conviction: _____
_____

Previous Residences	From (mo/yr)	To (mo/yr)
Street _____ City _____ State__ Zip ____	_____	_____
Street _____ City _____ State__ Zip ____	_____	_____
Street _____ City _____ State__ Zip ____	_____	_____

List your past three immediate supervisors (do not include present employer):

Name/Title	Company	City & State	Work Telephone:	Home Telephone

Are you currently employed? (If yes, answer a, b, & c)   Yes ___ No ___
a) Have you informed your immediate supervisor that you are seeking other employment?   Yes ___ No ___
b) Have you already given notice?   Yes ___ No ___
c) May we contact your immediate supervisor/present employer without jeopardizing your current position?   Yes *___ No ___
*If so, why? (e.g., plant closure, layoff announcement, etc.): _____

The information I have provided above is true and correct to the best of my knowledge.

Signature: _____   Date: _____

The Interview Itself

When I teach interviewing, I recommend the behavioral-based method of gathering information from the candidate. In this technique the candidate is asked to talk about specific achievements or situations in his or her work career. Sometimes this is also called behavioral-event or behavioral-incident questioning.

Behavioral interviewing is increasingly being used by employers. It emphasizes behavior, not general statements. By evaluating specific examples of past performance, interviewers can anticipate the candidate's future behavior on the job. Each candidate is asked to give an example of his or her performance. For example, when discussing attendance, you want the applicant to cite figures, as in the statement "I only missed one day last year, and was late three times all year."

This technique involves asking simple, probing questions until you can clearly see the situation or incident in your own mind. Make the applicant relate in vivid detail his or her specific achievements. In other words, get very sound evidence through examples, facts, statistics, and cases where and when such behavior occurred. Demand evidence for anything that is said. It's all based on the very simple premise that actions speak louder than words.

"Please give me an example." These are the five most important words in the interviewer's arsenal, and they can't be used too often. The main purpose of an interview is to gather stories—that is, practical illustrations of how things worked out (or didn't). You can almost measure your ef-

fectiveness by the number of "sagas" an interview produces.

Instead of asking questions such as, "Are you
a good leader?" or "Tell me about yourself," and
then listening to vague and self-serving generali-
ties, ask for specific achievements and accomplishments. For example, say to the applicant,
"Describe to me an actual situation in which you
were a strong leader," or "Tell me with specific
examples why you are better than the other people we are talking to." Continually probe with follow-up questions until you can clearly visualize
what you're being told. The key is to listen actively to understand what action was taken, and
then learn what the result was. This, in a nutshell,
is what behavioral-event interviewing is all about.

The Interview in Perspective

As we have already seen, a common mistake interviewers make is talking too much. As an interviewer, you must learn the art of engaging
another person silently. Remaining silent is difficult for most interviewers, but the general rule is
that the interviewee should do about 80 percent
of the talking.

A related mistake is that of adopting a free-
floating conversational interview style. This
allows the candidate to discuss her experience
largely on her own terms and makes it difficult to
compare candidates. For the purpose of comparing responses across individuals, it is therefore
best to use a semistructured approach in which
provisions are made for follow-up questions as
needed. A detailed inquiry or a persistent follow-

up on an initially general question can bring out critical information about the candidate.

Don't stop digging until you really understand. The best interviewers ask the dumbest questions. In any interview, the interviewer has the worse hand. When something isn't clear, go back over it until you fully understand what is being said. Remember, your job is to ask questions, which means any kind of question that is necessary to know the job candidate. Think small. It's the details of someone's work life you're after.

A detailed, semistructured interview should not be a stress-inducing exercise. Some managers conduct stress interviews, believing that this will allow them to observe how the candidate copes with stress. The problem is that in most cases, the stress produced by this approach is quite different from the stress produced by the job. A little anxiety in the candidate is fine, but deliberately setting up the applicant to feel unusual stress serves no good purpose.

As with a good detective, your purpose during the interview is not to make a friend but to get the facts. Keep asking the applicant to talk about what she actually did—her day-to-day activities, short-term or long-term projects, and ultimate achievements. Notice what she is wearing, her tone of voice, even when she smiles. When you finally go over the questions, you may be surprised at the patterns and clues that emerge.

Identifying and gathering references during the interview may be stressful for a candidate who has something to hide. Those who are good candidates will have no problem with this. In fact, they will see you as an interviewer who is in control and knows what you're doing. They will see it as a chance for you to hear from the many fine people they have helped and worked with. A poor applicant would rather keep control and steer you to the references of his choosing.

The interview is the best time to identify references. Squeezing every ounce of usable information you can out of the interview is just good time management. Any interviewing method that does not include identifying references is not in tune with what's needed today.

Finally, a word about interview impressions. Try as you may to conduct an objective evaluation, an interview is essentially an emotional event. Subjective reactions, whether conscious or unconscious, are inevitable. To clear up any doubts you may have, call those persons (references) who have been closely involved on the job with the applicant and who can provide further insight into the person. With this information, the odds are that you will make the right hiring decision.

Some companies are now using a separate background questionnaire that is completed by the applicant prior to the interview (see Exhibit 8-4). The purpose of this questionnaire is to get basic behavioral information from the candidate before the interview itself and thus save precious interviewing time. In addition, it tends to keep the interviewee honest. If a separate form is not used, you may want to ask some of those questions during the interview itself.

The short interviewing format (Exhibit 8-5) can be used to interview hourly or entry-level applicants. It has corresponding reference checking questions (short version), shown in Exhibit 12-5, that match the interviewing questions. These two

Exhibit 8-4. Sample background questionnaire.

LMN CORPORATION
109 Aurora Way
Denver, Colorado

Your background and work history will be discussed with you during your interview. Please answer all questions with a "yes" or "no" prior to the interview.

	Yes	No
1. Have you ever been placed on probation or terminated for poor job performance?	____	____
2. Have you ever been disciplined or fired for insubordination?	____	____
3. Have you ever been disciplined or discharged for violating a safety rule(s)?	____	____
4. Have you ever been disciplined or terminated for absenteeism, tardiness, failure to notify your company when absent, or any other attendance-related reason?	____	____
5. Have you ever been disciplined or discharged for theft, unauthorized removal of company property, or related offenses?	____	____
6. Have you ever been disciplined or fired for fighting, assault, or similar offenses?	____	____
7. Have you ever been disciplined or discharged for being under the influence of alcohol or drugs, or for the possession, use, or abuse of alcohol or drugs?	____	____
8. Have you ever been convicted of a crime?	____	____

I certify that the above answers are true to the best of my knowledge. I understand that any falsification discovered before or after I am employed may be cause for my being disqualified or removed from employment with the company.

_____   _____
(Candidate's signature)   (Date)

_____
(Social Security Number)

Exhibit 8-5. Interviewing questions (short form).

Look for someone you can be enthusiastic about. Beyond your gut feeling, make sure the applicant is qualified for your opening. Use these key questions for all the candidates you interview for the position.

- ▶ How long did you work for your last employer? Why did you leave? How about the employer before that [*go back at least 5 to 10 years*]?

- ▶ Specifically, what did you do for your last employer(s)?

- ▶ What were your accomplishments? What changed as a result of your being employed there?

- ▶ What are your strengths as you see them? Would your friends agree?

- ▶ What former bosses, co-workers, or subordinates can I call for references? [*Get at least five names*].

- ▶ What do you feel separates you from other applicants for our opening?

- ▶ What can we expect from you if you come to work for us?

A final word of advice. Use common sense, as you would for any kind of decision. Look for solid evidence that the person you choose can increase your unit's performance and really help your operation.

---

forms have been used with great effectiveness by many employers.

The long interviewing format (Exhibit 8-6) is appropriate for higher-level openings. Review these twenty questions and decide on those you want to use for the opening you have. You may

(*text continues on page 110*)

Exhibit 8-6. Interviewing questions (long form).

Explain to your candidate:

"I will ask you general questions that provide an opportunity for you to tell me your specific career achievements to date, as well as your future expectations. I am going to be concentrating on your relevant work experience, knowledge, and competence."

"I will also ask you to provide the names of references you feel will share with me their views regarding your career progress. This is important because I may want to contact specific individuals who can verify what we have spoken about during the interview."

Ask your candidate:

1. Why are you interested in this position?
   Subquestions (if necessary):
   √ How did you get into this type of work?
   √ Why are you interested in making a career move now?

2. What specific attributes do you possess that will make you effective in this position?
   Subquestions (if necessary):
   √ What unique talents will you bring to us?
   √ How much do you know about our position opening?

3. What is your definition of career success?
   Subquestions (if necessary):
   √ How will you know when you have become successful?
   √ What would you like to be earning in the years ahead?

Exhibit 8-6. (continued)

4. How has your previous job performance been appraised in terms of specific pluses and minuses?
   Subquestions (if necessary):
   √ What three areas of your job do you like the most? Least?
   √ What recent accomplishments are you most proud of?
   √ Whom can I contact to discuss this with (if needed)?
   Name _____ Phone _____ Company _____

5. Describe a situation in which you felt particularly effective?
   Subquestions (if necessary):
   √ What is the most important idea you implemented in your present/last job?
   √ What was your single most important contribution to your present/last employer?
   √ Who would have knowledge of this action (if needed)?
   Name _____ Phone _____ Company _____

6. Describe a time when you felt ineffective and explain exactly what you did about it.
   Subquestions (if necessary):
   √ What did you learn from this experience?
   √ What was the biggest mistake you ever made in your working career?
   √ Who would have knowledge of this occurrence (if needed)?
   Name _____ Phone _____ Company _____

7. What qualities have you liked or disliked in your previous bosses?
   Subquestions (if necessary):
   √ Who was the strongest boss you ever had? The weakest?

✓ Do you prefer to work for a delegator or for one who gives you close supervision?
✓ Who was your last boss? Can we contact him/her (if needed)?
Name _____ Phone _____ Company _____

8. How many employees have you supervised in your past assignment(s)?
What has been the group's overall level of performance?
Subquestions (if necessary):
✓ Describe how you influence or motivate others.
✓ Do you like being in charge of people?
✓ Who should I speak with to review this information (if needed)?
Name _____ Phone _____ Company _____

9. Have you had direct hiring authority? Have those you hired worked out?
Subquestions (if necessary):
✓ What do you look for in a job applicant?
✓ What do other people think about the people you hire?
✓ Who would have knowledge of this area (if needed)?
Name _____ Phone _____ Company _____

10. Give me an example of your having cut the costs, improved the efficiency, or eliminated unnecessary work in your daily activities.
Subquestions (if necessary):
✓ What was the most satisfying thing you ever did?
✓ Have you ever received an award or a citation?
✓ Who can I discuss this with (if needed)?
Name _____ Phone _____ Company _____

Exhibit 8-6. (continued)

11. Have you been a reliable employee? Can you give specific examples to illustrate this?
Subquestions (if necessary):
√ How many times were you absent in the past year? Year before?
√ How often have you changed jobs? Moved or relocated?
√ Who can I discuss this with (if needed)?
Name _____ Phone _____ Company _____

12. How well do you interact with supervisors, peers, and subordinates?
Subquestions (if necessary):
√ In what manner do you communicate with your subordinates? With superiors?
√ Describe a time in which you worked on a team or in a group and tell me what role you played in that group.
√ Who can I talk with about this (if needed)?
Name _____ Phone _____ Company _____

13. What would be the advantage to a new company hiring you?
Subquestions (if necessary):
√ Describe the best company you ever worked for?
√ What is the biggest single problem your current/past company had?
√ Who would be able to discuss this with me (if needed)?
Name _____ Phone _____ Company _____

14. What, in your opinion, is your future growth potential? How far can you go?
Subquestions (if necessary):
√ How have you changed over the past five years?

✓ What would other people say about your potential?

✓ Who would be the best person to talk with about this (if needed)?

Name _____ Phone _____ Company _____

15. How are you best managed?
Subquestions (if necessary):
✓ What do you expect from a manager?
✓ What was your favorite manager like?
✓ Is there someone who would be helpful to us in this regard (if needed)?
Name _____ Phone _____ Company _____

16. What is your single strongest characteristic? . . . and your greatest weakness? What are you doing to build on that strength? . . . and what are you doing to reduce the weakness?
Subquestions (if necessary):
✓ In what areas of your present job are you strongest? Weakest?
✓ In the past year, what classes, seminars, or conferences have you attended? How many were at your own expense?
✓ Whom may we talk with to better understand this (if needed)?
Name _____ Phone _____ Company _____

17. What mistakes have you made in your career?
Subquestions (if necessary):
✓ Have you ever been reprimanded?
✓ Have you ever been fired?
✓ Who would have knowledge of this area (if needed)?
Name _____ Phone _____ Company _____

18. What was the most difficult ethical decision you ever had to make?
Subquestions (if necessary):
✓ How do you define ethics?
✓ What is unethical behavior?

Exhibit 8-6. (continued)

19. Is there anything in your background that you are not particularly proud of, that you'd rather talk about now than have discovered during our reference checking?
    Subquestions (if necessary):
    √ What will your current/previous employer say about you?
    √ Have any of your employers ever refused to provide a reference for you?

20. Is there anything more you would like to contribute to the interview?

Advise the candidate:

"At times I may find it valuable to speak with other persons your references may refer me to. Are there any restrictions as to whom I may contact? If so, please explain why and give me their names."

Name _____ Company _____

Name _____ Company _____

decide to use some of the questions for a lower-level opening and all of them for a key position. Feel free to substitute or to add questions of your own. This form and the longer reference checklist in Chapter 12 provide the basis for a power interview and thorough reference checking.

Remember, the right questions, properly used and followed up on, will uncover the information you seek from a job candidate. Good questions are the foundation of a good interview.

9

Converting the Candidate Into Your Best Helper

Put the candidate to work for you. The applicant is totally under your control throughout the entire hiring process. You liked the résumé he submitted and selected him to come in for an interview. You asked the questions you wanted to, treated the candidate the way you wished, and decided how long to meet with him. The entire interview was in your hands, and the decision as to whether the applicant was a strong candidate was totally your decision.

Now, you usually let your control end here, and take on the full burden of contacting the applicant's references and getting whatever information you think you'll need to be sure of your hiring decision.

But I say, that's not the way to do it.

Instead, it is the candidate's responsibility to assist you, as necessary, to verify that the information about his or her work history is correct. Have the candidate contact the references you have chosen and ask them to speak freely with you. Then he should ask the references to call you or arrange a time for you to call them. In short, the candidate makes all the arrangements for you to talk with the references. Don't waste your valuable time doing work the candidate can do for you. Let the candidate chase down his references. Also, I sug-

gest having the candidate send his résumé to all
the references so that you can ask them if it's correct.

Now I know you're probably thinking,
"What about the person who goes to his three or
four best friends and sets them up to be the people I want to speak with?" His buddy Joe becomes the president of the company, Karen
becomes his immediate supervisor, Barry becomes a peer, and Dave becomes his subordinate.
To begin with, I can't imagine this being pulled
off successfully. With any astuteness on the part
of the reference checker, using unexpected and
thorough questioning techniques (which will be
explored in Part IV), this could never happen.
Good questioning will immediately stop this
farce dead in its tracks. Of course, you can always
call the reference back to verify that it was the person to whom you thought you were speaking.

If this still bothers you, then have the candidate call the reference to arrange a convenient
(and exact) time for you to contact the reference.
Whichever situation you choose, there is no reason that you should spend your valuable time
chasing down references when the candidate will
gladly do it for you. Why should you care how
the reference contact is made so long as you get
to talk to the person?

A New System

Maybe if we look at it from the standpoint of
what's in and what's out, it will become clearer:

What's In

▶ You tell the candidate what references you
want to talk with.

▶ The applicant contacts the references you selected and arranges a time to talk.

▶ You get the information you want from the reference and clear up any concern(s) you have.

▶ You are in total control of the reference checking phase of hiring.

What's Out

▶ The candidate tells you that such and such are the references you can talk to.

▶ You chase down the references the applicant has given you.

▶ The reference tells you what the candidate wants you to hear, and you accept it and don't go any further.

▶ The candidate keeps indirect control of the references you can speak with.

Does using the candidate as your helper work? Let me share just two of the many stories that have been related to me.

A Midwestern line manager explained that a few months earlier his company had been getting ready to hire a key manager and was quite serious about one particular candidate. When that candidate had asked how soon he could start, he was told that his references had to be checked first. The candidate then asked who the company wanted to speak with and was told the names of four people. The candidate volunteered, "If you would like, I can get hold of these people for you and have them call." Within three hours all four persons had called and the reference checking was completed. The line manager commented to the seminar group that it had never occurred to him to make this practice a permanent part of his employment system, but he was sure going to use it in the future.

An East Coast manager told me about how she was hired by her company six months previously. She was very excited about joining the company, but it took the company two weeks to check three references. In fact, after the first week, she had called to make sure that she was still in the running for the position. She was assured that she certainly was, but that her reference checks had not been completed. She said she thought to herself that she should offer to contact the references and ask them to call the employer to discuss her. She didn't think this would be appropriate, however, so didn't. She now sees this as a very sensible thing to do.

I can't tell you how much easier this new method has made things for those involved in the employment area. I have had line managers and human resources staff members tell me that this system has made the task of checking references immeasurably easier and quicker. It has literally been the single most important step they have taken in their careers, and it has made their jobs more enjoyable and their work more effective. I have been told by many that they now have time for a long lunch once in a while and can even go home on time.

Getting candidates to help you contact their references is really an obvious way to facilitate reference checking. It works because it's a win-win situation. The candidate gets the job right away, and you get your employment duties over with quickly. Good candidates with nothing to hide appreciate it, whereas poor candidates who want everything they say to be accepted without question don't like it a bit—because it's almost guaranteed to expose them. A strong candidate with a high energy level will more than welcome the opportunity to influence the hiring decision in his favor. If someone is too lazy to perform this task, you might well ask yourself: will she be similarly lazy on the job?

In fact, I have spoken to job seekers and recommended that they use the new system to their advantage as job candidates. I tell them that when they learn they are truly in the running for a position, they should immediately ask if their references will be checked. If so, they should offer to help contact the references in order to ease the burden on the employer and to speed up the process so they can go to work as soon as possible. It's a proactive approach that can help them be viewed as stronger and more viable candidates. Remember this yourself if you are ever on the other side of the desk as an applicant.

What Are the Advantages?

There are five definite advantages to using this new system:

1. By having the applicant ask a reference to speak with you, that person now becomes a personal reference. As you will see in Part IV, this is the only real way you will get consistent, in-depth reference information about your candidate.
2. It solves the legal question of obtaining a release from the candidate before asking

people to disclose personal information about him.

3. The applicant does not contact work for you. You don't waste your valuable time playing telephone tag and then pleading with someone to give you information.

4. It greatly speeds up the hiring process, possibly preventing the loss of a good candidate because you took too long to make your decision.

5. The applicant will see you as someone who is in control of the situation, and your company as one that is very thorough and selective in choosing new employees. This will make him feel good about going to work there.

How Honest Are You?

We have discussed how important it is to insist on and get honest answers from job applicants. But honesty is a two-way street. Are *you* being honest with your prospective employees? Whether it is unintentional or deliberate, misinforming candidates is a mistake recruiters should not make. You should tell candidates what they need to know to make an informed, conscious decision, not what you think they want to hear.

Candidates know—sometimes sooner, sometimes later—when a company hasn't been on the up-and-up with them. They will catch on, and when they do, the result may be as simple as a job offer rejection or as complex as a lawsuit. Misrepresentation claims are brought against former employers often enough to be a potentially costly problem.

For example, say you ask an applicant why he left his last job and he says, "I couldn't stand my boss. He was dictatorial, never had a good word for anyone, and cursed at people." Now if this describes almost exactly what his new boss in your company will be like and you don't tell him, what do you think will happen when he comes to work for your company? Or let's say you have a sales opening and you tell the applicant that you have salespeople who earn $100,000 a year and that there is no reason she can't be at this level too. What you don't tell her is that there are just two salespeople at this income level and they are the owner's sons who have been given all the old and really large accounts. In actuality, the average salesperson earns about a quarter of this after the first year, and is lucky even to make a living for the first six months.

Many times, managers, in their eagerness to fill a vacancy, oversell the job and company. It is easy to find yourself saying things like, "This is a great company to work for," or "You'll really like it here." The anxious applicant wants to believe this, and when someone is hungry, everything looks appetizing. Once hired, though, reality sets in. There is nothing wrong with praising your company, but when you are making the job and company appealing to an applicant, stick to the facts. Describe a typical workday, and be sure to describe the company culture the way it really is. New employees are quick to figure out when they have been misled about the job, and may quit as a result.

Deal with firing guidelines. Managers spend

a great deal of time telling applicants what qualities and abilities are needed but neglect to outline
what is not acceptable. In addition to explaining
what qualities you are seeking, tell the applicant
what the company won't tolerate. Be honest about
the downside, even though you may find it pain-
ful to do so.

Promises made during job interviews can
lead to litigation later. There have been suits by
fired employees who believed they were misled
about conditions at a company before they accepted a job there. From both a moral and a legal
standpoint, it's best not to exaggerate opportunities or conditions at the company during interviews with prospective employees.

Advice for the Job Candidate

Upon being considered for a solid job opportunity, you don't want to lose out because of a poor
reference contact. Although reference checks may
be beyond your control, you can manage what is
being said about you by choosing your references
wisely, keeping them informed about your employment situation, and briefing them prior to receiving any phone calls.

Select your references in advance. Carefully
choose people who are knowledgeable about
your abilities and performance. This means current or former managers, peers, subordinates, and
clients. Identify those you think will make positive observations and comments about your work
history and accomplishments.

Once you understand the company and its

requirements, offer the names of appropriate references who can help you get the new position. References are a great asset to obtaining a new job, so use them wisely. Your references should be able to properly comment about your work. If the potential position involves customer contact or sales, past customers and suppliers may also be useful as references.

Try to select people with good communication skills who can and will converse with someone about you. People who are hard to reach, unclear, or evasive may hurt your efforts. Provide their full names, where they are employed and the position they hold, and both their work and home telephone numbers.

Advise your references that they can expect to be called about you. Try to find out the name of the person who will be calling and give this information to your references. It is best to keep your references informed about the progress of your job search. Provide them with copies of your résumé, and tell them how your interview went. By doing this they will be better prepared to tailor their remarks to best support you. If someone is hesitant about being your reference or does not seem to understand what is needed, replace that person with a more suitable reference.

By company policy, most firms will give little or no information regarding current or past employees. If your current or past employer prohibits its managers or others from providing references, contact former managers, co-workers, and subordinates who have joined other firms or who have retired and ask them if they would be willing to be a reference and provide a recom-

mendation regarding you. Also, if you are currently employed and want your search to remain
confidential, you will have to contact people from
earlier employers who knew you and ask them to
be a reference for you.

In fact, I personally go so far as to recommend that, as a candidate, you ask all potential
employers if they will provide a reference on
your performance with their company in the
event that you leave or are released. Advise a new
employer that you intend to work very hard to be
a top performer and expect that this information
(or whatever report they have about you) will be
relayed, if requested, to a potential employer. If
the hiring officer says that the company won't say
anything good (or bad) about you, you may want
to consider a more progressive company that
won't just file away those important years of your
personal life and career.

If you have had a negative or poor relationship with a former company or manager, you
may want to address this situation during the interview. It is best to be honest and straightforward in explaining a situation or period of
employment that just did not work out. By doing
so you may be able to turn a negative situation
into a positive opportunity by being straightforward and honest about what has occurred in the
past.

Remember that prospective employers will
want to ask questions and clarify any concerns
that they have. Often what isn't said is more important than what is said. Encourage your references to be open and honest about their past

association with you. You can anticipate that questions will be asked regarding your strengths and weaknesses. The areas that will probably be explored are your communication skills, ability to get along with others, adaptability, reaction to pressure, and ability to do your work. Most good firms will check your references. If discrepancies or problems exist, you may be eliminated from consideration for employment.

Your references are part of your employment search. Maintain and cultivate these relationships. It is best to develop references throughout your career so that when you need them they will be available. You need to have references who are knowledgeable, prepared, and enthusiastic. A good reference will dramatically improve your chances of landing a new job.

Collaboration With Mutual Gain

There is a very simple and obvious reason why the new system will work for everyone concerned. Getting a new employee or a new job should be a win-win scenario. The company gets a good employee; the employee gets a good job. The hiring process is a way to meet both these needs. Both parties stand to gain, and both parties are winners.

So what are your options? You can take the position that it's just too difficult to check someone's references and forget about doing it altogether. You can do it the old way, trying to track down the references yourself and then hoping they'll speak to you. Or you can try the new way, as many have, and enjoy the tremendous results it produces. It's a system designed to help the good candidate, not a way to protect those who don't want their work record checked.

Part III Summary

There is a new way to contact references that you should be following to maximize the effectiveness of your work. In this part of the book you discovered that:

- ▶ Most job seekers believe that whatever they say will probably never be checked out.
- ▶ When shown that their past record and performance will be checked, most job candidates immediately see the need for being truthful.
- ▶ Usually interviewers just can't take the time to track down and convince references to share with them the information they have about an applicant.
- ▶ The candidate who really wants the job will do anything reasonable the interviewer asks to assist the hiring process.
- ▶ Based on these observations, there is no reason not to have the prospective employee contact the references you want to speak with and make all the arrangements for your reference contact.

Part IV

Reference Checking Techniques That Work

10

How to Get Reference Information–And How Not To

Information flows in a predictable way. There are very effective and workable methods for getting people to speak with you about someone they know. In fact, they are so obvious that you might even say they're not really techniques. Yet, I assure you, most people trying to check references don't realize these techniques exist, let alone use them.

Before getting into exactly what these techniques are, let's look at how information about employees, both past and present, is usually exchanged. Information flows back and forth on two levels, formally and informally. There is no way that information can be controlled on the informal level. One friend talking to another about someone they both know is one example, as is a manager talking to another manager about a present or past employee, or one employee telling another employee what he or she really thinks about someone with whom they both work. It's two people talking about a third person, which is a perfectly normal occurrence. That's the content of a good part of our daily conversation. Then why is it so terrifying when we talk about someone we are thinking of hiring?

When you stop to think about it, checking references is a very natural thing that we all do at times. We talk to other people whenever we are thinking about a new doctor or auto repair place or when taking trips or going to a new restaurant. We don't think twice about asking people who have been there what they have experienced. If you're going to spend a lot of money, in building a new addition to your house, you had better talk to knowledgeable people about how well a contractor has performed for them. It's just the sensible thing to do.

Now, let's look at the formal path for exchanging information between organizations and the people within them, that is, at what takes place when one company legally or officially requests information from another company. Getting an official statement from a company is usually a complicated and difficult task in which the right officer(s) has to be involved. We all know that this process takes a lot of time and patience.

On the formal level, under tight controls, a limited amount of information is exchanged. At the informal level, however, there is virtually an unrestricted flow of information. The primary difference is that one method functions in keeping with a rigid company policy whereas the other circumvents that policy. While personnel departments can confirm employment dates, job titles, and rates of pay, the best sources of information about an applicant's work habits are his former supervisors, peers, and subordinates. It's really that simple and basic.

Let's look at how this works in the employment situation. If you call supervisor John Doe at XYZ Company and ask him about someone who used to work for him, chances are you won't learn much because he has to follow his company's policy on not releasing such information. But if the candidate gives the same supervisor, John Doe, as his personal reference, and you call and advise Mr. Doe that he has been given as a personal reference for the applicant, the chances are that he will see the situation in a wholly different light and cooperate fully with you.

Under the formal method you get little or no information because of legal or other fears, such as possibly giving the wrong information or not representing the company properly. With the informal method, you will probably get natural and insightful comments and observations that can be quite valuable. Obviously, of the two roads to travel, the informal one is most likely to get you where you want to go.

The real reason the formal road is painfully slow to travel is that it's a case of one company trying to talk to another company, which is virtually impossible. You don't call companies—you call people. The informal road is easier to traverse because it's one person talking to another person, the only way things get done (see Exhibit 10-1). To be a good reference checker, you have to take the "open road."

Difficult as reference checking is now, it's worth the effort. A few questions to the right people can help weed out the candidate who handles interviews well but performs poorly on the job. It can also highlight good employees who aren't adept at interviewing. And if you can't get references on a candidate, look for someone else.

Why Give References?

There are some very good business and common-sense reasons for giving reference information on

Exhibit 10-1. Two roads to travel—informal and formal.

INFORMAL

METHOD	PATTERN	RESULT
Friend to Friend	Unrestricted flow of information	Insightful comments and observations
Manager to Manager	Not controlled	Very valuable
Employee to Employee	Avoids company policy	
OPEN ROAD—SOME DETOURS		

FORMAL

METHOD	PATTERN	RESULT
Personnel department to Personnel department	Very limited amount of information	Little or no information
Company to Company	Rigidly controlled per company policy	Limited value
ROADBLOCKS		

former employees. Yet I am always amazed at how often these reasons are ignored or overlooked, even by human resources professionals and business managers who should know better. These reasons include:

▶ *Giving references continues company-paid outplacement assistance.* Companies paying for expensive outplacement assistance for a former employee who was fired or released due to downsizing often won't cooperate with another employer who may be interested in hiring this person. I actually called a company that was paying in the range of $20,000 for outplacement assistance for one of its separated executives, and was told it couldn't provide any information about the individual. Paying for such professional help and then hindering the process when the unemployed person's job-seeking efforts start coming together hardly makes sense!

▶ *It lowers unemployment costs.* Unemployment rates in most states are based on how long former employees are unemployed and have been drawing unemployment assistance. The quicker these individuals get back to work, the lower your unemployment tax rate will be, so why not cooperate fully with a new employer who may put the unemployed person back into the work force?

▶ *It ends an unpleasant situation.* When someone is terminated, for whatever reason, it's tough emotionally on everyone involved. Unemployed people are often not happy and tend to look backwards, blaming their last employer for not fully appreciating or using their talents. The previous employer is trying to get on with business and let bygones be bygones. The easiest way to make this happen is to help ex-employees find new jobs.

▶ *It provides a reward for good performance and a penalty for poor performance.* Let's suppose someone who worked for you over the past ten years was a very loyal, productive, and reliable employee who always received top performance ratings; however, she had to be released when the firm reorganized. Another employee, who was employed approximately the same amount of time but had a bad attitude, low productivity, and high absenteeism, was also let go, which was something you had wanted to do for a long time anyway. If someone were to call you about these two people, and under your company policy you aren't allowed to say anything, it could be concluded that both had the same level of performance. The top employee does not receive any credit for being good and the marginal employee is not penalized for her poor work record. What could be more unfair?

The Real World

In fact, the policy of not giving out reference information about a past employee, established by the human resources departments of nearly every company, is ignored by most people. I can tell you as an experienced reference checker that people really want to provide information about someone, whose record they know; you just need to give them a good reason and make it easy for them to do so. When I contact references, I get cooperation about 95 percent of the time. No more than one in twenty fails to respond or help at all. Although the rules of the game set by most companies forbid talking about someone's personality and performance, most people will not play this game.

If one of your company's executives meets an executive from another company at the local country club (where they both have company-paid memberships) and is asked his opinion about someone who used to work at your company, do you think he will reply that he can't say anything due to your nondisclosure policy, and that the other executive will have to call human resources? Or, if one of your foremen meets a foreman from another company at the bowling alley (where they are both on company-sponsored teams) and is asked about a former employee of yours he is thinking of hiring, do you think your foreman will cite company policy and tell him to call personnel? If you do, you are suffering from a bad case of naïveté and have lost touch with the real world.

The overwhelming majority of people will be honest with you if you ask them the right questions. I personally received a call concerning a person I had worked closely with at a large Fortune Top 50 company. I was asked to talk about him and responded by giving his strong points, both professional and personal. Never once was I asked if he had any shortcomings or areas that needed improvement. Yet there were some and, if asked, I would have explained them. Indeed, I would have said that I would not hire this person! But I was not asked. It's like the joke in which someone asks another person if he will be a character witness for him and is told: I will tell them you're the biggest character I know.

There are three basic premises that apply to the world of reference checking:

1. The chances are overwhelming that a person will not—
   —perform any better
   —work any harder, or

    —behave differently for you than he or she has done for others in the past.

2. The most powerful tool in business is information because good managers, given good information, can make good decisions. When making an all-important hiring decision, you need the best information you can get.

3. In the long run, instincts are no match for information. There is a no more certain recipe for disaster than a decision based on emotion.

The Positive Aspects of Checking References

I truly believe that the real basis for success in checking references is a positive feeling about the task on the part of the person doing the checking. Unfortunately, most of those assigned to checking references don't like doing it. At the beginning of my seminars on the subject, I ask how many participants really enjoy checking references. Naturally, I raise my own hand, but out of a group of fifty or more, I usually find no more than two to three people who also enjoy doing it.

As I see it, the problem is that it's hard to be good at something you don't enjoy doing. Unless I can show you that checking references is a very positive action, and that you can actually have fun doing it, you won't be very successful. A negative feeling about something you are trying to do is immediately transmitted to others, and this feeling is probably why most people who attempt to check references are not successful.

What are the positive aspects of checking references?

1. *Reference checking provides clear testimonials to support your decision to hire a particular person.* Let's face it, if the references check out, you'll feel much better about your judgment.

2. *It gives justice where justice is due.* In other words, you'll hear good things about good people and poor things about marginal performers. Good people are penalized when we don't hear what others have to say about them.

3. *It may provide additional evidence of accomplishments or reveal factors that were not covered in the interview.* Every time I check references on someone, I hear favorable points about the person that weren't brought out during the interview, such as he's a good family man, she's very religious, he doesn't smoke or drink, she's not a substance abuser, he runs three miles every day, and so on. Yet these factors reflect well on the applicant and would otherwise be missed.

4. *It gives management-development advice that enables you to best fit the person into your organization.* Everyone has flat spots, and if you're doing a good job checking references, you will discover them. It has often been said that our greatest strengths are also our greatest weaknesses. For example, if someone is very aggressive, you need to look at the other side and learn how sensitive he is to others. If someone works very hard and puts in long hours, she may not be a good delegator.

A reference check I conducted on a candidate for the position of plant manager (who at the time was an assistant plant manager with another company) indicated that he was totally dedicated to his work, usually working ten or more hours a day and four to five hours on Saturdays and Sundays. All four of the references I contacted felt that he was a great manager who was very effective; however, they also said he had better slow down before he had a heart attack. They all commented that he really needed to learn to delegate more. When he started the new job, he was told what his best friends had said about him, and this had quite an impact. In fact, he and his new supervisor developed a plan of action to change these personality and management flaws.

The more you know about someone in advance, the better you will be able to help him or her succeed in your company. What you learn about someone up front is only what you will find out three months, six months, or a year or so after he or she has been working for you. Isn't it better to discover it sooner rather than later and proactively address the situation, not just react later on?

5. *Effective reference checking establishes you as someone who can protect your company from a poor hiring decision.* A company invests a considerable amount of time, money, and energy in hiring and training a new employee and if, for whatever reason, the new person doesn't work out, the cost skyrockets. An employee who fails and leaves after a few months can cost a company anywhere from $5,000 for an hourly worker to $75,000 for a manager in lost productivity and money spent on training, to say nothing of lowered morale and profits. If you can sit in front of a hiring manager and present solid facts and opinions to support

the hiring decision, you will be viewed as a valuable member of the company.

I am a firm believer that you won't be effective at checking references unless you see the positive side of it. All the techniques we are going to look at in the coming pages won't make you very effective in this function unless you believe you are doing something necessary and positive for your company, as well as for the candidate. No one gains from a poor hiring match, and, in particular, the reputations of those who let it happen will suffer.

Types of Checking

There are two types of background checks: the record check and the reference check. The record check determines honesty. The record check is one that can be performed by secretaries or clerical personnel to determine whether the information the applicant has supplied is accurate. It is nothing more than confirming that the previous dates of employment, job titles, academic degrees, professional license(s), and such on the applicant's résumé are accurate. In fact, the people who relay this information may never have met the person in question. Unfortunately, this is as far as many companies go in their checking. They may call it reference checking, but this is a misnomer.

The reference check determines competency on the job. This phase of checking gets into candidates' ability to conduct themselves appropriately as well as to do their job, and is usually carried out by the employment staff or hiring manager. It

involves an in-depth conversation with someone
who knows or has worked with a particular candidate. It gets into one, two, or three areas of personal conduct, depending on how far you want to
go, with an increasing level of difficulty the further you delve into the person's background. The
three areas are:

1. *Sociability:* How well does the candidate
   get along with and relate to other people?
   Information on this issue is fairly easy to
   discover and discuss and can usually be
   obtained from anyone you speak with—
   both personal and professional references.
2. *Work habits and ability:* How well does the
   applicant know his work and perform on
   the job? You want to assess the person's
   technical or functional ability, and also his
   attitude on the job. Obviously, this information has to come from people who have
   worked with the person, such as fellow
   employees, peers, subordinates, supervisors, or company officials.
2. *Personal character:* What is the candidate's
   basic personality, including morals and
   ethics? This level of information may be
   desired for a key or very sensitive position
   and will have to come from talking not
   only to work associates but to close
   friends, secretaries, or neighbors as well.
   In fact, it may move beyond normal reference checking into a private investigation
   or a background investigation for a security clearance.

Based on my personal survey of seventy-two
major companies in the Midwest together with re-

sponses to questions on the subject of depth of background checking of job applicants raised at seminars, I found that 58 percent of companies conducted both record and reference checks (see Exhibit 10-2).

Exhibit 10-2. Depth of checking undertaken.

11

New Reference Checking Techniques

Creative reference checking gets results. The most progressive human resources executives agree on the importance of checking applicants' backgrounds. The issue just can't be ignored anymore. They find ways of obtaining references despite "no-talk" policies. As businesses nationwide struggle with this situation, many are finding that, with creativity and persistence, effective background checking is still possible. A positive attitude about checking references, coupled with good techniques, will produce wondrous results.

The Basic Contact

Before we get into the specific techniques that will make you a successful reference checker, let's take a look at the basic reference contact itself. I'm sure by now you're convinced that you should contact the references you choose, not just the ones the candidate suggests that you contact. Additionally, you can develop new references from the references you do contact. There is no law anywhere that says you must limit your contacts to those references the applicant has listed or wants you to speak with.

Let's take the case where you have spoken with a number of references, and then a new reference points out something of concern. For example, you called the first reference and there were no special problems. You talked with reference number two, and she also said everything was all right. Then you call reference number three, who indicates that the applicant was absent from work a lot, possibly owing to a chemical abuse problem for which he eventually underwent treatment. Now most reference checkers would immediately think that they should call some more references to get a handle on this—which you may do.

However, there is another way to check out "new" information. You have already established a telephone relationship with the two earlier references, so why not call them back, remind them of your initial contact, and tell them that something has come up since your first conversation on which you need to get their views? Then explain the issue to them. You'll be surprised how quickly they'll tune in and try to help you, because in a way you're putting them on the spot and testing their basic credibility. Contacting references a second time to clarify questionable information that has subsequently come to light is a sensible, yet underused, reference-contact method.

Another often overlooked problem is that you can't see what the reference is doing at the time of your call. The reference is probably doing his or her job, and your call is an interruption and nuisance no matter how much they want to help you and the candidate.

But you can lessen the feeling of intrusion simply by asking permission to talk, for example, by saying:

- ▶ "Is this a convenient time to talk?"
- ▶ "I will need about twenty minutes of your time. May I continue?"
- ▶ "With your permission, I will ask you a few short questions."

The worst thing your references can say is no. But since you've asked permission, they will more likely answer affirmatively. If they do say no, they'll probably be more willing to answer your follow-up question, which is: "When is a good time to call back?" "Wednesday, mid-morning" might be the response. You must then be organized enough to record this telephone appointment in your tickler file.

If you call the reference at the appointed time and she tries to beg off your phone conversation, gently remind her that she said she would talk to you at this time. If she still wishes to end the conversation, you can try rescheduling it. But by asking permission, you've transferred the decision to the reference, and you are more likely to be successful.

Getting sufficient time to speak with a reference is a frequent problem. A typical reference call may last ten to forty-five minutes, a significant slice out of someone's workday. Therefore, it may be necessary or advisable to call references at home during the evening or over a weekend to get the information you want. There is usually a noticeable difference in the way people respond when they're at home. They are more natural and relaxed and can give you the uninterrupted time you need to discuss the candidate in question. Most people at work are under heavy time pressure and may also be afraid of being overheard because they feel they're representing their company rather than speaking personally about the candidate. You don't get good responses when someone's mind is somewhere else. Therefore you need to eliminate all the distractions you possibly can.

Occasionally, I have spoken with references at work and then had to finish the conversation after they returned home; I've found that it is almost like talking to two different people. At home, people are more responsive to my questions and are often more willing to elaborate. It's always better to have too much time rather than not enough. In my private reference checking practice, I make about 30 percent of my calls after working hours and on weekends to people at home. I never hesitate to call anyone at home—in the evenings, on weekends, or holidays—and have never run into any resentment of my call.

Now, I realize that those who work a normal workday can't spend all their evenings and free time contacting references. However, in special cases and for critical openings, it may be important to make that sacrifice for your employer. An employment manager at one of my seminars said that because they are so much more effective, she encourages her staff members to make after-hours reference calls, and gives them compensating time off for doing so. She added that she can tell if they have put in the time by the content of the reports they submit to her.

Introducing Yourself With Impact

When making your initial contact with a reference, you should take charge quickly because the

first inclination of the person may be not to participate in the reference contact if there is a way out
of it. The reason for this reaction is the negative
legal aura that has surrounded reference checking
and the resulting fear that "you can get into trouble for what you say." Additionally, most people
would just as soon not get involved in a discussion about someone they know for fear that what
they say might get back to that person. So, like
it or not, there is an almost instinctive fear about
serving as a reference for someone who is looking
for a job.

The way to start your reference contact is to
tell the person that the candidate (by name) has
asked (if that's the case) or authorized you to contact him or her as a personal reference in order to
obtain a new job. The term *personal reference* is a
trigger word that usually gets someone's instant
cooperation. For help in visualizing this introduc-
tory sequence, please note the accompanying
work script in Exhibit 11-1. Explain to the reference that a job offer will not be made until you
can verify the candidate's background. In most
cases, this is all you need to say to get the reference's cooperation. If this doesn't work, there are
other useful statements you can make (see script).

Another way to get cooperation is to ask the
reference if he would like a personal call from the
candidate authorizing him to speak to you. About
80 percent of the time, the reference will tell you
that this won't be necessary because he doesn't
want to bother the candidate or alert him to his
reluctance to speak with you. I find that most people agree to start talking after I make this statement. You might tell the person that her
unwillingness to speak with you must mean that

Exhibit 11-1. Introduce yourself with impact.

If Reference Answers:
▶ Mr./Ms. _____, my name is _____ and I'm with XYZ Company.
▶ We are in the process of hiring _____. And before we will extend an offer, we need to check his/her background.
▶ He/She has asked that we contact you as his/her *personal reference*.
OR
▶ He/She has given us approval to speak with you as his/her *personal reference*.
▶ I would like to spend a few minutes with you. Is this a convenient time to talk? If not, when would be the best time/day? At work/home?
▶ I will call you then.
OR
▶ I will look forward to your call. Thank you.
If Reference Is Not In:
▶ This is a personal call. When will he/she be in?
▶ Please have him/her call me at _____.
OR
▶ A friend of his/hers has given him as a personal reference and I need to speak with him/her as soon as possible. When should I call him/her?
If Reference Will Not Cooperate:
▶ Would you like the candidate to call you and personally authorize you to speak with me?
▶ Should I assume that your unwillingness to speak with me means that it would be a bad reference?
▶ Does your refusal to talk about the candidate apply only to this person or to all former employees?
▶ I must explain that unless we can talk to people who know the applicant, there may not be a job offer.
Fallback (Comment):
▶ I can't understand why we're having a problem getting you to talk with us, because we're just trying to help _____ get a new job. Who can I talk with to clear up this matter?

it would be a bad reference. Then let the reference defend her position. You can further ask if her refusal to talk about the candidate applies only to this particular candidate or to all former employees.

Another way to find out about past work behavior is to look into the applicant's reason for leaving the company by asking if he/she is eligible for rehire. Normally, you won't have trouble getting an answer to this request.

As a last resort, you might pressure the person to cooperate by advising the reference that by not speaking with you he could be held legally liable for the candidate not getting the job. Sound farfetched? It isn't! I have personally advised people who had a previous employer who would not speak about their employment at the company to consider taking legal action against that employer for interfering with their efforts to get a new job—and I think you may see more of this as a reaction to employer nondisclosure policies.

There is always a final fallback position, which involves exclaiming that you can't understand why you're having a problem getting the reference to speak with you, because all you are trying to do is help someone she knows get a new job. Then ask who you can talk with to clear up this matter.

Taking Charge Quickly

Once you reach the reference contact, take immediate control to ensure that the time spent both by you and the reference is not wasted but instead produces meaningful information. One very important point must always be kept in mind, however. When you call people on the phone you are literally interrupting them at some point in their daily activities, and you must always try to adjust to where they are at the moment.

All of us have a scale of emotions we go through in a given day ranging from being happy to being stressed out, and might include everywhere in between. You will be making contact with a reference somewhere along this emotional scale, which you won't know beforehand, and you have to be sensitive to where he or she is at the moment. For example, if the person you contact has just come out of a difficult meeting with her boss, she may be nervous and not fully focused on your call. On the other hand, if she has just come out of the boss's office after receiving a big raise, you will probably have a much more cooperative reference. See the point? You will be catching everyone along some point in the emotional continuum, and you must learn to adjust quickly.

This is common knowledge among salespeople and others who deal with the public all the time; however, it may not be fully recognized by those strictly administrative types of people who are paid to process information as quickly as possible. They tend to see all their tools, and even other people, as simply a means to getting their job done. Always remember that when you ask someone to be a reference, this person is doing you a favor. Politeness counts, and you must always keep this in mind. Also, be sure that *you* are in the proper emotional state; when you're upset, you don't see things as clearly.

The following rules may help you to reach

your goal of getting a reference to cooperate with you:

1. *Expect the most of the references you call.* Remember, you are sincerely trying to see your company and the candidate come together. Be absolutely surprised when someone doesn't cooperate.
2. *Be relaxed, calm, and courteous.* Remember, you are asking someone to give you his or her valuable time.
3. *Explain the purpose of the call.* Tell the reference that an offer cannot be made until references are checked, and that the candidate has asked or authorized you to talk with him.
4. *Ask permission to continue the call.* Inform the reference, "I will need about ten (or twenty) minutes of your time. Is this a good time to talk?"
5. *Expand your information.* Start with verification questions, then move on to performance, developmental concerns, and networking questions, which are covered in more detail in Chapter 12. Continually probe to gain insight.
6. *Don't assume anything.* Listen reflectively and ask for clarification and intent. Learn exactly what the reference is telling you. It's much better to have too much information than not enough.

The Voice's Body Language

You can often detect enthusiasm or the lack of it if you pay attention to "voice language." What is said obviously is important, but even more important is *how* it's said or what is *not* said. We have all been around long enough to know that body language really communicates a person's innermost thoughts to us. Well, the voice does the same thing.

Talking on the phone deprives us of visual clues, but it makes it easier to detect language and voice clues and to ask direct questions. Also, being on the phone makes the other person more comfortable. It's much easier for people to talk when they don't have to face you.

When checking references, never assume anything. If you're not sure of something, continue to probe until you feel that you are being told everything you need to know about the subject in question and that you understand it thoroughly. If you don't understand something, continue to ask questions until you can actually visualize the answer you are being given. If the information is not forthcoming, ask for more information or clarification, with follow-up questions such as, "Would you please give me some examples of his accomplishments in that area?" "Please explain that further." "I'm having a hard time understanding what you're telling me, and need to stay on this subject." Ask follow-up questions in your own language and style. But the point is not to stop asking questions until you are sure that you understand totally what you're being told. Above all, don't allow yourself to be "snowed" or misled about a candidate's real qualities and qualifications.

In my private reference checking practice, I have run across some strange and fascinating answers. In one instance, I asked if the candidate was honest. There was a long pause, and the reference answered, "As honest as the next person." I then asked, "How honest is the next person?" After another long pause came the reply, "As honest as most of us." What I finally sensed was that I had a dishonest person trying to cover his own and the candidate's unethical behavior. My favorite answer is, "He was too light (or too heavy) for that." Finally, after hearing this answer so often, I started asking if the reference thought that the candidate didn't weigh enough (or weighed too much) and needed to change his diet. After laughing, the reference will explain in more exact terms what he or she really means, that the person was either overqualified or underqualified for the position. I was once told that a candidate had left the company because of "organization dynamics." When I asked the reference to explain what he meant by that phrase, I found out it meant that the applicant couldn't get along with other people in the company.

Returning Your Calls

How do you get references to return your calls? What you generally have to deal with here are voice mail messages and gatekeepers that shield references from you. There is no 100 percent, surefire way to reach people who aren't in or available, but there are a few things you can do to increase your chances.

Leaving a Voice Message

Be ready to leave your phone message. Know exactly what you're going to say. Leaving a strong, articulate message will create a positive impression and may earn you a return call. A weak, bumbling message can create a negative impression and may stop a return call. Also, leaving a strong message can help to warm up the reference once you make voice contact.

Leave a voice message something like this: "Mr. Brown, this is Sally Cole with XYZ Company. The reason I'm calling is that someone you know has given us your name as a personal reference. [*If the applicant is no longer employed there, you may want to give his actual name.*] "Please call me at [*your tel. no.*]. You may call me collect, if you wish. The time/date is [————]. I need to talk with you at your earliest convenience. Thank you."

Dealing With a Gatekeeper

If an assistant answers, you should leave a message similar to the one above. This assistant is your way of reaching the reference. Make the screener feel important. Sometimes you will find that he or she also knows the applicant and thereby becomes an additional reference contact. You may even get valuable information from this contact that the original reference wouldn't reveal. Don't let the opportunity pass without learning something. If you reach a real person, not just a recording, ask questions. Treat the gatekeeper with the same courtesy, professionalism, good humor, and sincerity you would use with the reference.

Voice mail and gatekeepers are in maximum use during regular business hours. So try calling before or after work hours or on weekends. The reference may be working then, answering his own phone. And the higher you go, the nicer they are.

In short, be creative, make you point, and relay the message you want to leave. Of course, if you're using the new system of your applicant having the references call you, you won't have these contact problems, will you?

Letters of Recommendation

Letters of recommendation are becoming increasingly unreliable as a means of evaluating job candidates. In all but the rarest cases, a letter is favorable, even when the writer knows the candidate is mediocre or unqualified. How many negative letters of reference have you seen? This is so because the writer knows the candidate will read the letter and perhaps even sue if the contents are not to his or her liking or are insufficiently substantiated.

When checking references, do not rely on these written documents. The references were probably written at the time of termination, and the employer, feeling bad about it, laid on the praise. Also, such a letter can be faked.

Let's say that one of your employees has decided to pull up stakes and relocate to another part of the country. Because he doesn't know what companies he'll be applying to, he asks you for a letter addressed "to whom it may concern" to attach to his résumé. You can now do one of three things: (a) Write a glowing reference, sign it, and send him on his way; (b) ask him to write the letter, then review it, change a few minor points, and return it; or, more advisably (c) tell him a reference letter is too impersonal and that you'd much rather talk to prospective employers so you can tailor your comments to their job requirements. There really is no better way to give reliable information about a candidate than to speak personally with the prospective employer.

The Reference Circle

References will lead you to other references. Exhibit 11-2 illustrates the circle of references and how it widens outward. Normally, you will start with the references the candidate gave you or,

Exhibit 11-2. The reference circle.

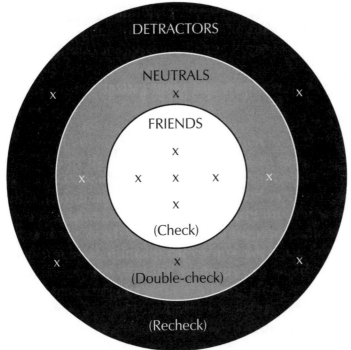

preferably, with the references you have identified during the interview as people you want to
speak with about the candidate. This is the inner
circle of people close to the candidate, with whom
the candidate may have spoken and perhaps even
prepped as to what they should say. However,
these references can lead you to the neutrals, that
is, people who will freely express their views—
good or bad—about the candidate. And they, in
turn, may even point out detractors, people who
don't like or get along with the candidate.

The way to get this to happen is simply to ask
at the end of each reference contact whether the
reference can think of or recommend anyone else
with whom you should speak. Believe me, that's
all there is to it, and it works. It's nothing more
than the simple networking of your reference contacts. Then, of course, based on the particular situation, you can decide if you want to make the
additional contacts.

Networking references is the most effective
way to go after the special information you want
or to keep from being blindsided by a prearranged reference. And, as you have seen, there is
no law in any state that says you have to talk only
to the references the candidate has given you. You
can continue the process for as long as you feel
it's necessary.

Some recruiters even ask if there is anyone
the candidate does not want contacted, and his
or her reasons for not wanting such individuals
approached. Exhibit 11-3 illustrates such a request, which you may want to add to your employment application form.

Exhibit 11-3. Do not contact form.

At our discretion, we will be contacting people you have worked with in the past.

Is there any reference(s) you do not wish us to contact? If so, please explain why.	DO NOT CONTACT
	Name _____ Reason _____ _____
	Name _____ Reason _____ _____

Nobody's Talking

What happens when, no matter how hard you try, you just can't get people to talk about a job candidate? Do you give up and take the line that many line managers and employment specialists take, that because checking references is so difficult and usually doesn't work, it should be abandoned as part of the employment process?

Believe me, with a little extra initiative, you can make reference checking work for you and get the information you need to make a proper hiring decision. The following actions should help:

1. *Expand (and raise) your contact level.* If you don't want in-depth information about someone, call the human resources department. Its job is to enforce the company's no-information policy. A personnel department usually won't give you

anything beyond the former employee's dates of employment, previous job title, and possibly confirmation of the last salary earned, sometimes doing this only in writing. In many cases, HR staff members have never worked with the candidate and may never even have met him. You know at the outset that this may happen, so don't be surprised when it does.

Obviously, what you have to do is expand your contacts to key members of the company who have worked with the candidate. These can be subordinates, peers, or supervisors. I can tell you from years of experience that this is all you have to do. I can also tell you that the higher people are in the organization, the easier they are to talk to. In fact, upper managers act as if they don't even know that there is a company policy against giving out information about former employees or people who currently work for the company. In most instances, they will freely discuss and comment on the strengths and weaknesses of the person in question, all in a very courteous and helpful way.

2. *Make use of high-level executives.* They instinctively know that the exchange of information is a vital aspect of business life; they also sense that there are good business and commonsense reasons for giving references. Obviously, you need to stick with people who either personally know or have worked closely with the candidate, but that's the only limitation you have. Don't call the chairman of a company about everyone who has ever worked there. But do call him if the candidate reported directly or even indirectly to him.

The former president of a company that was sold to an overseas firm and dissolved mentioned to me that he personally told about twenty key employees to feel free to use him as a reference when attempting to land a new job. He said he received only one phone call regarding a former member of the company. I can assure you that high-level people are always ready to help someone get ahead. That's why they are where they are.

In fact, when I have problems with personnel staff specialists or line managers who don't want to cooperate, I frequently call the top human resources officer and explain my dilemma. Almost without exception, he or she will direct me by name to someone within the company. When I call that person, I mention who suggested I contact her, and she is then very willing to talk to me.

3. *Check your own employees.* You may be surprised to learn how often you have employees who know or have worked with the candidate. During the interview, when the candidate is willing to tell you anything you want to hear, ask if he knows anyone who works at your company. Write down their names, and, especially if you're with a large company, you may have all the reference contacts you need without having to make an outside call. Some companies have added a special section on their employment application form where employees who know the candidate can be identified (see Exhibit 11-4).

4. *Confront the candidate.* What if information just isn't flowing back to you, but you're still interested in a certain applicant? Go back and advise the candidate that you have a problem, that you can't offer her a job until you have satisfactorily checked her references, and that unless some-

Exhibit 11-4. Contacts within the hiring company form.

Do you know anyone employed by the company?	☐ YES ☐ NO
If yes, give name of employee(s)	

thing can be worked out, she won't get the position. Then, together with her, identify references and determine how to get them to speak to you. As mentioned earlier, have her do the work for you in tracking down and inducing these people to talk with you. A good candidate will welcome that role.

"Don't Call My Employer"

In my national seminars, the question is always asked, "What do I do when the candidate is currently employed and I can't call his employer because it will jeopardize his present job?" I always point out that any time someone is in the job market, he is taking a calculated risk that his present employer may find out he is looking. However, I agree that in such a case you certainly don't want to do anything that would jeopardize his current job.

The solution is rather easy. With the candidate, identify persons with whom he or she worked at the company who are no longer there, such as those who have recently left for new employment or who have recently retired. Every company has some turnover. There are also customers, clients, and even vendors who can be contacted. Additionally, you would be surprised how often fellow employees and even the person's supervisor know he is looking for a new job. If you ask the candidate, he will usually be able to supply the names of current fellow employees who can be relied on not to spill the beans.

The use of former employees or retirees as references is an excellent practice today. Companies have unloaded thousands of people who can readily be contacted. Because they are no longer connected with the company, they are usually more than willing to talk freely and openly about someone with whom they used to work. I find I am using these people more often as references; in fact, in some cases, they have been my primary source of reference contacts. I have noticed that retirees will often talk your arm off, because you are talking about their old job and comrades, subjects that are usually near and dear to them.

You don't have to and should not ignore your reference checking responsibility just because someone is currently employed. With a little initiative on your part, the situation can be properly handled. There is never a reason not to check someone's references.

Getting Personal

Remember, every reference is a "personal" reference because everyone you talk with knows the candidate personally! As mentioned earlier, to be effective you must talk with references on a person-to-person basis. Virtually none of them will give you the official company position on someone they know; however, they can certainly give you their personal view.

The best way to get such person-to-person connection is to stress when introducing yourself that the candidate has named her as a personal reference, if that is the case, or that the candidate has authorized you to talk with his personal references. Everyone you speak with knows the candidate personally, and they are speaking only for themselves.

Many employment specialists advise against using references provided by the applicant because they are most likely to be friends of the applicant who have been programmed to say only favorable things. I personally don't agree with this line of thinking and believe these people can be very valuable sources of information for the following reasons:

1. *Most people don't want to get involved in lying, even to help a friend.* I am convinced that, with a few exceptions, people aren't comfortable lying and certainly don't want to lie for someone else. If you ask the right questions, they will be honest with you. In fact, I have actually had personal references named by the candidate tell me that something the candidate said was false or badly misleading. Even personal friends often go out of their way to set the record straight.

2. *Personal references are usually not prepared for unexpected questions.* No matter how well rehearsed a personal reference is, he or she can't have an answer ready for every probing question a good reference checker will ask.

3. *Personal references will lead you to the neutrals and the detractors* (refer back to Exhibit 11-2).

As mentioned earlier, this circle of references can quickly take you to other people who also know the candidate, even to those who don't think that highly of him or her.

4. *Personal references can provide special information about the applicant.* Sometimes there is an important concern about the candidate that needs to be cleared up, such as possible personal problems, family instability, bad habits, or to what extent previous difficulties have been resolved. For example, if you're getting ready to relocate someone to a new part of the country, you would do well to explore how friends think this will affect the candidate's family situation.

I once performed a reference check for a major company that was getting ready to hire a young woman who had a very high-paying job in San Francisco. She was now willing to go to work in a small city at a much lower salary. Talking with her friends, I quickly discovered that she was dating a young medical doctor in the new town and fully expected that they would be married soon—and wanted to concentrate her full attention on this relationship. With this information in hand, her willingness to move made a lot of sense. I have also frequently been asked to try to determine whether an applicant still has a chemical-dependency problem, which I find his or her friends to be very frank and open in discussing.

Telephone Tips

I suggest trying what I call the "exact-time" method for calling people, which I use with great

results. This involves, whenever possible, estab-
lishing an exact time to talk and then calling back
at precisely that time. In other words, if I'm calling someone or making a return call, I advise the
person of the specific time I will call. I tell her, or
the person who is scheduling calls for her, that I
will call at a certain time, emphasizing that when
her phone rings at that time it will be me.

You would be surprised how often the person I'm calling is literally sitting by the phone
waiting for my call. There have been times when,
for some unavoidable reason, I wasn't able to
make the call at the time I said I would; and when
I called later, I was told in no uncertain terms that
I hadn't called when I promised and that the irri-
tated person was sitting by the phone or had al-
tered his or her schedule in anticipation of my
call. Believe me, this exact-time method can really
save time and is much more efficient for you as
well as for the person you're calling. Try it for all
your calls, business and personal; it will save a lot
of time and reduce your frustrations with having
to play telephone tag.

When you're calling people, you need to
make it easy and enjoyable for both yourself and
your respondent. In my private reference checking practice, I call all over the country and
throughout the world. I have a big map of the
United States on the wall of my office in front of
my desk. When I call a particular location, I mentally travel to that spot on the map. I may ask
briefly about local happenings or the weather,
thereby taking advantage of my chance to speak
with someone who is there. I do the same thing
on international calls by swinging around to my
back wall, which has a world map with time

zones. It's my way of traveling every day and enjoying the work I do. I truly believe this makes me a more enjoyable and interesting caller.

References by Mail, Telephone, or in Person

The best way to gather background information about someone is to visit the reference and have a face-to-face discussion. I have done this on rare occasions and it is highly productive, although it takes a lot of time. Author/businessman Harvey Mackay said in his book *Swim With the Sharks Without Being Eaten Alive*, "*I interview candidates in their home setting with their spouse and children. I want to see the candidate's personal values at work in the most revealing setting. It's also a great integrity test. Does the candidate's home life match the description in the interview?*"*

The next best, and most practical, way is to telephone using the practices and techniques outlined in this book.

In my view, the least effective way of checking references is to spend time writing letters. It is both time-consuming and seldom productive of much information. Those companies and people who do it by mail are probably more administrative-minded than results-oriented, or, as one of my seminar participants said, are taking the cowardly way to perform their background-checking responsibility.

Efforts to check the applicant's background by mail may be futile. Previous employers may be slow in answering the queries you solicit through

*(New York: William Morrow, 1988), p. 199.

the mail. Or they may not answer at all. Studies have shown that the return rate can be as high as 56 percent and as low as 35 percent. The reason for the overall low return rate is that many employers are concerned that former employees may take them to court over information written on a reference form.

Another problem is that it takes too long, usually two or three weeks, to receive a reply. If you are trying to hire special categories of applicants who are in short supply, candidates just won't wait for you to go through this long and involved process.

You are far better off checking references by phone. You get more comprehensive information and spend less time and effort. However, for the categories of information outlined in the following section, you may have to use the mail.

Searching Public Records

Record checking such as checks for criminal convictions, worker's compensation awards, credit standing, and driving violations are lawful if done properly. There are several simple rules employers should follow before implementing these checks to ensure that their companies are not exposed to potential legal liability or other problems.

Criminal Records Checks

Federal law does not prohibit criminal records checks. Employers inquiring about convictions on a job application form should make it clear that a criminal conviction will not automatically disqualify the applicant from employment. Some state laws have restrictions on utilizing criminal records in making employment decisions. Check the state laws to ensure that you are in compliance with their requirements.

Worker's Compensation Records

The Americans with Disabilities Act prohibits an employer from asking an applicant prior to an offer of employment whether he/she is disabled or about the extent of the disability. Thus, the prudent course of action is to make the job offer contingent on the applicant passing a physical examination or medical screen, which then could involve a check on the applicant's medical and worker's compensation history.

Credit Reports

Inquiries about financial status and credit rating should be limited to situations where there is a clear business necessity for the check. This is a touchy and not well-defined area in which there are no clear guidelines. As with arrest and conviction records, the Equal Employment Opportunity Commission (EEOC) has concluded that a policy of failure to hire because of poor credit status has a disproportionate "adverse impact" on minorities.

Driving Records

When operating company vehicles or equipment is an important or essential part of an employee's job, the employer has a legitimate interest in the applicant's driving record. The Americans with Disabilities Act authorizes such inquiries only when driving is an essential function of the job.

"Leave the Driving to Us"

Trying to verify the credentials and checking the employment background of a job applicant is a time-consuming problem and headache for most managers. To help companies make reliable hiring choices, a number of firms devote themselves to the special niche of reference reporting.

Although some human resources professionals believe an employer should call a candidate's references personally, others prefer the objectivity and timesaving benefits offered by an outside firm. Many feel that when you are the interviewer and have a vested interest in the candidate, you may not want to ask the hard questions that will challenge your opinion or decision.

Although expensive, the use of a commercial service to investigate applicants may be especially desirable for higher-level, key, or sensitive positions. A good commercial service has the additional resources and will spend the extra time to check into an applicant's background to an extent that might not be feasible for the individual employer. These firms are experienced in conducting in-depth reference checking and preparing a full report about each candidate. It can be worthwhile to get their input before extending a job offer.

When I started my firm in 1988, there were only a handful of full-time reference checking specialists in the country. Now, by my last count, there are hundreds of such firms. Exhibit 11-5 lists those that have been around awhile and seem to be well established.

The Fair Credit Reporting Act

The Fair Credit Reporting Act contains several disclosure requirements for the use of "consumer reports" provided by consumer reporting agencies. New amendments to the federal Fair Credit Reporting Act (15 USC 1681, et seq.) that went into effect on October 1, 1997, apply to reference checking.

Unquestionably, reference checks are consumer reports and investigative consumer reports under the FCRA. A consumer report is any summary of an individual's credit standing, creditworthiness, general reputation, personal characteristics, or "mode of living." An investigative consumer report is the obtaining of this information through personal contacts. This broad definition brings almost all outside background checks under the scope of the statute.

Before a consumer report may be obtained from a consumer reporting agency, the employer must: (1) provide the employee or applicant with a clear and conspicuous disclosure (in a document that consists solely of the disclosure) that a consumer report may be obtained for employment purposes; and (2) obtain written authoriza-

Exhibit 11-5. Reference checking firms.

- ▶ Advanced Information Research
  Owings Mills, Maryland
- ▶ American Background Information Services, Inc.
  Stephens City, Virginia
- ▶ Avert Inc.
  Fort Collins, Colorado
- ▶ Barada Associates, Inc.
  Rushville, Indiana
- ▶ CARCO Research
  Smithtown, New York
- ▶ Career Tracers
  Cocoa Beach, Florida
- ▶ CDB Infotek
  Santa Ana, California
- ▶ Certified Reference Checking Co.*
  St. Louis, Missouri
- ▶ CIC, Inc.
  Bellair Bluffs, Florida
- ▶ Citadel Investigation, LLC
  Paramus, New Jersey
- ▶ Corporate Investigations, Inc.
  Pittsburgh, Pennsylvania
- ▶ Corporate Solutions, Inc.
  Hudson, Ohio
- ▶ Credit Reporting Information Services, Inc.
  Livonia, Michigan
- ▶ Dependable Report Services
  Martinex, California

- ▶ Edge Information Management, Inc.
  Melbourne, Florida
- ▶ Employment Research Services
  Atlanta, Georgia
- ▶ Employment Screening Associates
  Chicago, Illinois
- ▶ Equifax Employment Service
  Atlanta, Georgia
- ▶ Faxworld
  Phoenix, Arizona
- ▶ Greet America Public Record Services
  Dallas, Texas
- ▶ HR Plus
  Evergreen, Colorado
- ▶ The Industrial Foundation of America
  Houston, Texas
- ▶ InfoLink
  Tarzana, California
- ▶ Information Resources
  Redondo Beach, California
- ▶ Information Services Network
  El Segundo, California
- ▶ Inter-Fact, Inc.
  Cleveland, Ohio
- ▶ IRSC, Inc.
  Fullerton, California

*The author's firm.

▶ Clarence M. Kelly and
  Associates, Inc.
  Kansas City, Missouri

▶ Peter Levine Associates
  Framingham,
  Massachusetts

▶ McGraw-Hill/London
  House
  Rosemont, Illinois

▶ Melendez & Associates
  Santa Ana, California

▶ Moore Information
  Services, Inc.
  Long Beach, California

▶ Myers Research &
  Consulting Inc.
  Stow, Ohio

▶ National Employment
  Screening Services
  Tulsa, Oklahoma

▶ National Resource Services
  Richardson, Texas

▶ Omniafax, Inc.
  Tampa, Florida

▶ Pinkerton Service
  Corporation
  Charlotte, North Carolina

▶ Pre-Employment
  Screening, Inc.
  St. Louis, Missouri

▶ Proudfoot Reports
  Incorporated
  Melville, New York

▶ Records Search, Inc.
  Ft. Lauderdale, Florida

▶ Reid Psychological Systems
  Chicago, Illinois

▶ Transport Protective
  Association
  Rancho Palos Verdes,
  California

▶ Trans Union Employment
  Screening Services, Inc.
  Chicago, Illinois

▶ USDatalink
  Baytown, Texas

▶ James E. Van Ella &
  Associates, Inc.
  Chicago, Illinois

▶ Vericon Resources, Inc.
  Atlanta, Georgia

▶ Verifications Incorporated
  Minneapolis, Minnesota

▶ Verified Credentials, Inc.
  Burnsville, Minnesota

If I have omitted anyone, I am sorry. Please send me the names and addresses
of these firms so that I can include them in future publications.

tion from the employee or applicant. A sample
disclosure form is shown below in Exhibit 11-6.

If an employer doesn't hire the candidate as
a result of information contained in a consumer
report, the employer must provide that person

Exhibit 11-6. Sample disclosure form.

DISCLOSURE

We hereby notify you that a consumer report, including an investigative consumer report containing
information as to your character, general reputation,
personal characteristics, and mode of living, may be
obtained for employment purposes as part of the
pre-employment background investigation and at
any time during your employment. Should an investigative consumer report be requested, you will have
the right to demand a complete and accurate disclosure of the nature and scope of the investigation requested and a written summary of your rights under
the Fair Credit Reporting Act.

Please sign below to signify receipt of the foregoing
disclosure.

_____   _____

Signature   Date

---

with (1) notice that he will not be hired; (2) the
name, address, and telephone number of the consumer reporting agency that furnished the report;
(3) a statement that the consumer reporting
agency did not make the decision to take the adverse action and is unable to provide the consumer with the specific reasons why the adverse
action was taken; (4) notice of his or her right to
obtain a free copy of the consumer report within
60 days; and (5) notice of his or her right to dis-
pute the accuracy or completeness of the report
with the consumer reporting agency. See Chapter
13 for additional information on the subject.

12

Power Checklists and Questions

Ask the right question, worded the right way, at the right time. Doctors use questions to diagnose diseases; detectives use them to solve crimes; lawyers use them to defend clients; teachers use them to educate children; salespeople use them to satisfy customers. Questions are the workhorses of the mind. Without them, mankind's progress would come to a halt.

We have all heard the expression, "If you don't know where you're going, you'll probably end up somewhere else." This is eminently applicable to information gathering. If it's not crystal clear in your mind what you want to learn, you probably won't learn it. You can't just shoot the breeze with someone and then wonder why you didn't get any meaningful information.

Asking the right questions is more than half the battle in gathering reference information. Every question asked during a reference call makes a statement about how good you are at gathering background information. The quality of your questions ultimately will determine the quality of the answers you receive. The questioner is always in control. A common misconception is that the dominant party in a dialogue is the one who does the most talking. Actually, the opposite is true.

One of the major problems most companies have in gathering outside reference information is their telephone questionnaire forms. In most instances, these forms are simple checklists that are used for all reference contact calls—business, personal, and customer. In addition, such forms usually contain a lot of questions with narrow lines for writing in the answers, requiring the reference checker to fill in the blanks. Using these forms is basically stressful.

Before proceeding to what I have found to be a more useful and less stressful way to ask for and record reference information, it's probably best to review the legal aspects of checking references.

1. *Be sure you have the candidate's written authorization to verify his or her personal and employment history and other information affecting an employment decision.* This is normally included as part of the sign-off on the application for employment or the special form reviewed earlier in the book.
2. *Follow the checklist exactly to obtain the necessary information and opinions.* Obviously, each call will be somewhat different, but you should proceed in a preplanned sequence for consistency and thoroughness.
3. *For equal opportunity employment compliance, be totally consistent.* That is, ask all references the same questions, and never ask different questions of different groups (e.g., women, minority members, the handicapped).
4. *Report exactly what the reference said.* Do not try to interpret the message. If necessary, dig deeper or consult other people for the exact meaning of what you are hearing.

Penetrating the Mind of Someone Giving a Reference

Do you want to know what references are really thinking? Try this: Imagine references as onions. When you talk with them, all you see is the outer skin. But the truth is at the heart of the onion, and you have to peel away the different layers to find it.

Let me illustrate.

Suppose you ask a reference "How was John's attendance record?" The reference replies, "Not bad."

At this point, you may be inclined to go on with your questioning, thinking that you now have the pertinent information. In fact, however, you have engaged in only a very superficial level of conversation. You've been held to the outer part of the onion, and are still far from the truth.

Now it may be true that John's attendance was "not bad." But what does that answer really mean? It doesn't give you enough information to go on, does it? You need to direct the conversation to a deeper level.

The way to get deeper and more meaningful information is quite simple. Just question the answer to your previous question or ask for further clarification.

So, when the reference says, "Not bad," you say, "How many times was he absent and how many times was he late in the past year?" The reference pauses a moment and responds, "Well, he probably missed a couple of days a month and was late about once a week."

Now that's a little more information, isn't it? It's more detailed and relevant. But it's not deep enough. So you respond, "Were you happy with his attendance?" The reference says, "No, we talked to him about it." You then ask, "Was there any improvement in his attendance record?" The reference replies, "Whenever we talked to him, he would get better for a while but then would slip back into his old ways."

At this point, you have penetrated to a deeper layer of truth—a level that can make a real difference. You now have excellent information on which to base your all-important hiring decision.

Compare that to the reference's superficial reply, which you may have been tempted to accept. But you chose to dig deeper with a second question. Finally, at the third level, you sought and got a truly significant answer.

Getting to the deeper layers of truth isn't easy. It requires a certain skill in asking questions. You must develop the courage to dig for the answer even though it's easier just to accept what you're told and move on. The benefits of "peeling away the onion," however, are well worth the effort.

All successful reference checkers ask a series of questions in order to encourage the reference to reveal critical information about the candidate. They then probe deeply enough to get the "hard information." It has been my experience in supervising, training, and working with hiring managers and employment specialists that they generally don't look deep enough.

I know that the majority of reference checkers will stop pursuing information after the first question, and thereby see only the surface of the onion. A small number will ask a second-level question. And the best ones consistently probe further to get to the heart of the onion, where the truth really lies.

The reference will not simply volunteer the critical information. It must be carefully extracted by getting to level three, or the heart of the matter, as often as possible.

Some Good Tips

Because we talk too much, we listen poorly. If you truly want to listen better, don't talk so much. Nature abhors a vacuum and someone's words will rush in to fill the void. If they are not yours, they will be those of the reference. The person who talks will monopolize the conversation, while the person who listens will control the conversation.

If the reference you call just won't cooperate in any way, there is one last fallback technique that can make your call worthwhile. Describe the new company and the job the candidate will be performing. Ask the reference for his opinion as to whether this position sounds right for the applicant. You will be surprised how often the person will give you his view on this question. Then, at least, your time has been productive rather than wasted.

Always start your reference checking with education. I've found that about one out of twelve job candidates inflates or falsifies his or her education qualifications. With few exceptions, you can verify school attendance and degrees attained over the phone. Call your own school to see how easy it is to get this information. If you find a discrepancy in this area, you may not want to proceed any further. If you do, you'll already be alert to the possibility of fraud.

Look for extremes and their opposing side. For example, the biggest flaw that many aggressive people have is that they tend to take on more tasks than they can handle and end up dropping the ball on many of them. Or they may not be sensitive to the needs of others. Another example would be workaholics, many of whom have not learned how to delegate properly. Any time you note an overwhelming strength, turn the coin over and see what you find. In many of us, our biggest strength can become our biggest weakness.

I had a reference ask me to read back what I had picked up from what he said to me. I had no objection and did so. He listened and commented that my interpretation was correct and in fact complimented me on my good listening and thoroughness. This has happened to me only a couple of times in over thirty years of making reference calls. You would think that more references would want to be sure that what they have explained and commented on is, in fact, being understood and recorded properly by the reference checker. Again, we seem to have lost a lot of our common sense in the area of exchanging and explaining background information.

Reference Checklists

At the end of this chapter, you will find some sample checklists (Exhibits 12-1 through 12-4) to help guide you in calling references. There is a separate sheet for each type of reference contact—

Exhibit 12-1. Business reference checklist.

Candidate	Person Contacted
Potential Position:	Position: _____
Job: _____	Company: _____
Company: _____	Location: _____
	Bus. Tel.: _____
	Home Tel.: _____

QUESTION   RESPONSE

VERIFICATION

1. I'd like to verify _____
   dates of employment
   from _____ to _____.

2. What type of work
   did _____ do?
   (Title/general duties?)

3. Were _____ earnings
   $_____ per _____?
   Were there any bonus
   or incentive plans?

4. Why did _____
   leave your organiza-
   tion?

PERFORMANCE

5. What are _____
   strong points on the
   job? What characteris-
   tics do you most ad-
   mire about him/her?

Exhibit 12-1. (continued)

QUESTION	RESPONSE

6. Did _____
   supervise other peo-
   ple? How many? How
   effectively? Can he/she
   create a team?

7. What are _____
   shortcomings? Was
   there anything he/she
   was trying to change
   about him/herself, or
   should be trying to improve on?

8. How would you rate
   _____ job
   performance on a
   scale of 1 to 10 (10
   being high) compared
   to other people you
   have observed in a
   similar capacity?

9. Have you seen _____
   current résumé? Let
   me read you what it
   says were his/her du-
   ties and accomplish-
   ments with your
   organization. (Stop at
   each significant point,
   and ask the reference
   for a comment.)

10. Is _____
    honest?

QUESTION	RESPONSE

11. How well does
_____ relate
to other people?
Which employees
does he/she work best
with: superiors/peers/
subordinates? Is he/she
a team player?

12. How did _____
last job performance
review go? What
strengths were cited?
What recommended
improvement areas
were noted? How
about the perform-
ance review(s) prior to
that?

13. What did _____
accomplish with you?
What changed as a re-
sult of his/her involve-
ment? Did he/she
progress in the com-
pany?

14. Is _____ a re-
liable person? Does
he/she have any per-
sonal problems or bad
habits that interfere
with job performance?
Were there ever any
punctuality or atten-
dance problems?

Exhibit 12-1. (continued)

QUESTION	RESPONSE

15. If you could hire _____ today, would you do it? Is he/she eligible for rehire? If not, why?

DEVELOPMENTAL

16. What is the biggest change you've observed in _____? Where has there been the most growth?

17. Is _____ in the right job/career? How far can he/she go?

18. If _____ asked you what one thing would most improve the way he/she performs on the job, what specific advice would you give him/her?

19. What is the best way to work with _____ to quickly maximize his/her talents and effectiveness for the Company?

QUESTION   RESPONSE

NETWORKING

20. What other person(s)
    know _____?

Name: _____   Name: _____
Title: _____   Title: _____
Location: _____   Location: _____
Telephone: _____   Telephone: _____

OVERALL RATING:
  Excellent ☐ Good ☐ Some Reservations ☐ Poor ☐
Checks made by: _____ Date: _____
Comments/Summary:

_____

business, personal, or customer—as well as one
for contacting someone about hourly employees.
They have to be different for each type of contact
because the flow of questions varies. The questions in these sample forms were predesigned for
the type of reference being contacted.

Note that these reference-calling forms are
laid out differently from the ones used by most
companies. In these, the questions are on the left-
hand side; the right side serves as a work space.
When information is coming in fast, it is necessary to be able to write freely, to draw arrows con-
necting related information, or to circle important
facts. It's a lot easier and more natural than trying
to fill in the blank spaces on a tightly printed
form. In one of my seminars, a woman pointed
out that this made a lot of sense to her. She had
been using a yellow pad next to her company's

Exhibit 12-2. Personal reference checklist.

Candidate	Person Contacted
Potential Position:	Position: _____
Job: _____	Company: _____
Company: _____	Location: _____
	Bus. Tel.: _____
	Home Tel.: _____

QUESTION   RESPONSE

VERIFICATION

1. How long have you
   known _____?
   What is his/her rela-
   tionship to you?

2. How often do you see
   (or talk to) _____?

PERFORMANCE

3. What is your opinion
   of _____
   character, dependabil-
   ity, and general repu-
   tation?

4. What would you say
   are _____
   strong points?

5. What specific personal
   trait or skill is
   _____ trying
   to improve on?

QUESTION	RESPONSE

6. What basic values
   does _____
   hold for him/herself?

7. Does _____
   have any personal
   problems or bad habits
   that you ever noticed?

8. Is _____ honest?

DEVELOPMENTAL

9. What is the biggest
   change you've ob-
   served in _____?
   Where has he/she
   grown the most?

NETWORKING

10. What other person(s)
    know _____?

Name: _____   Name: _____
Title: _____   Title: _____
Location: _____   Location: _____
Telephone: _____   Telephone: _____

OVERALL RATING:
   Excellent ☐ Good ☐ Some Reservations ☐ Poor ☐
Checks made by: _____ Date: _____
Comments/Summary:

Exhibit 12-3. Customer reference checklist.

Candidate	Person Contacted
Potential Position:	Position: _____
Job: _____	Company: _____
Company: _____	Location: _____
	Bus. Tel.: _____
	Home Tel.: _____

QUESTION   RESPONSE

VERIFICATION

1. How long did _____ call on you? Did he/ she open your ac- count?

2. How often did _____ call on you?

PERFORMANCE

3. When _____ was calling on you, did you purchase less, more, or about the same amount?

4. How would you rank _____ performance com- pared with other sales- people who call on you?

5. Were you satisfied with the way _____ serviced your account?

QUESTION	RESPONSE

6. Was there anything
   that _____
   did, or did not do, that
   pleased you? . . . or
   displeased you?

7. Did _____
   keep you abreast of
   what was happening in
   the industry?

8. If _____
   were again to be call-
   ing on you with an-
   other company, would
   you be pleased/dis-
   pleased/neutral?

DEVELOPMENTAL

9. What is the biggest
   change you've
   observed in _____?
   Where has he/she
   grown the most?

NETWORKING

10. What other person(s)
    know _____?

Name: _____   Name: _____

Title: _____   Title: _____

Location: _____   Location: _____

Telephone: _____   Telephone: _____

OVERALL RATING:
   Excellent ☐ Good ☐ Some Reservations ☐ Poor ☐
Checks made by: _____ Date: _____
Comments/Summary:

Exhibit 12-4. Hourly employee reference checklist.

Candidate	Person Contacted
Potential Position:	Position: _____
Job: _____	Company: _____
Company: _____	Location: _____
	Bus. Tel.: _____
	Home Tel.: _____

QUESTION   RESPONSE

VERIFICATION

1. _____ said
   that he/she worked for
   you from _____
   to _____ as
   a _____. Is
   this correct?

PERFORMANCE

2. How often did you
   observe _____
   on the job?

3. What was _____
   attitude? Did he/she fit
   in with the other
   workers?

4. Was _____
   attendance OK? How
   often was he/she late
   or absent?

5. Is _____
   honest and reliable? Is
   there any evidence to
   the contrary?

QUESTION	RESPONSE

6. Does _____ have any personal problems or bad habits that interfere with job performance? Was he/she safety-minded?

7. What were _____ strong points? Weak points?

8. How productive was _____? How high are his/her quality standards?

9. How much supervision does _____ require? How fast does he/she learn?

10. Why did _____ leave? Would you re-hire him/her?

OVERALL RATING:
  Excellent ☐ Good ☐ Some Reservations ☐ Poor ☐
Checks made by: _____ Date: _____
Comments/Summary:

---

reference checking form to give her plenty of room to write. She then transferred the information onto her checklist when she had the time. In my opinion, any method that involves rewriting the information gleaned is just too inefficient and time-consuming.

When calling references, the flow of questions might be right. For this reason, the placement and wording of the questions on my sample calling forms have been tested and retested to maximize their effectiveness. For example, the checklists start with simple verification questions, then move on to performance-related information, then to developmental opinions, and finally to networking your reference contacts. I have tried whenever possible to use indirect questions—that is, questions that get the desired information without requiring the reference to give a personal opinion or explanation. Note that there is a space in each question to use the applicant's name.

In Exhibit 12-5, there is a separate form entitled Reference Checking Questions (short form), which corresponds exactly to the Interviewing Questions (short form), in Exhibit 8-5 in Chapter 8. The perfect match between questions on these two different forms makes for quick and efficient reference checking.

The more information you ask for, the more you will get. And if you don't ask, you don't get. It's that simple. I can't tell you how often I have received positive feedback on these questions. It is not unusual for references to make such comments as, "That's a good question," or "You are really making me think," or "I'm writing that question down to use myself."

The Business Reference Checklist (Exhibit 12-1) warrants special explanation mainly because it is the one you will probably use the most.

Let's look at what I consider to be key questions on the Business Reference Checklist, and why I have found them useful.

Exhibit 12-5. Reference checking questions
(short version).

---

*You have selected someone you are enthusiastic about.
Now verify that what you have been led to believe is in
fact true and accurate. Use these key questions for all the
references you contact about the candidate.*

- ▶ How long did _____ work for your company? Why did he/she leave? [*Go back at least five
  to ten years.*]
- ▶ Specifically, what did _____ do for you?
- ▶ What were _____ accomplishments?
  What changed as a result of his/her being employed there?
- ▶ What are _____ strengths as you see
  them? Would other people agree with you?
- ▶ What other people (supervisor, co-worker, subordinate) can I call about _____? [*Get at
  least one more name.*]
- ▶ What do you feel separates _____ from
  others doing the same or a similar job?
- ▶ What can we expect from _____ if he/
  she comes to work for us?

*A final word of advice: Use common sense, as you would
for any kind of decision. Look for solid evidence that the
person you choose is, in fact, the person who can increase
your in-house capabilities and really help your operation.*

Question No. 9: "Have you seen [John's] current résumé? Let me read you what it says were
his duties and accomplishments with your organization."

If you remember nothing else from this book,
remember this technique. If you suspect that the
candidate's résumé is inflated or wrong, read it to

the reference. This has worked innumerable times for me and for other people who have used it. If there is an error or lie on the résumé, the reference will tip you off by his or her reaction, sometimes even laughing at how out of line it is. And this person will tell you what it should be. You can also use this when someone just will not participate in giving you reference information. Ask if you can at least read to him what John said on his résumé. Usually, the reference contact will agree and then will make valuable comments about what's stated on the résumé.

When you really look at it, someone's résumé basically says, "This is where I worked, here is what I did, and this is how good I was." These three statements are usually made for each place where a person has been employed.

One of my favorite stories involves a situation where I suspected that what was on an applicant's résumé was not accurate. I asked a reference whether he minded if I read to him what the applicant had stated on his résumé about his employment at the company. I paused after each sentence to see if there was a response from the reference, but there was nothing but laughter. Finally after reading the ten-sentence description on the résumé, I asked, "Is there something wrong?" The reference requested that I stay on the line while he went to get his boss.

The boss came on the line, and I reread the résumé's description to him. Now there were two people laughing. I asked again, "Is there something wrong?" The boss said that what I had been reading was really a description of his (the boss's) job, and that the résumé was all wrong. In fact, the boss said, "If he was that good we would have hired him for my job."

Question No. 12: "How did [John's] last job performance review go? What strengths were cited? What recommended improvement areas were noted? How about the performance review(s) prior to that?"

Why try to reinvent the wheel? If you're talking to the applicant's previous supervisor, rather than asking for an opinion about the candidate, why not have him or her relay what was reported on the last performance review? It doesn't require any new judgment or opinion, so there should be much less resistance to providing this information. Ask if the employee was given a copy of the performance report. If so, you may want to have him bring it in for your personal review.

Question No. 18: "If [John] asked you what one thing would most improve the way he performs on the job, what specific advice would you give him?"

I can sense when the reference doesn't want to tell me something unfavorable about the candidate. However, I know that this question will help uncover the information. I find that references are very open, helpful, and honest in answering this question.

The Personal Reference Checklist (Exhibit 12-2) for use with someone who knows the candidate only on a personal basis, but has not worked with him, is self-explanatory and appropriate for this type of relationship.

The Customer Reference Checklist (Exhibit 12-3) is for contacting someone on whom a sales applicant has called. The questions fit this type of business relationship and will produce very valuable information.

The Hourly Employee Checklist (Exhibit 12-4) is designed specifically for reference contacts on hourly employees. I developed it for a major corporation that wanted to get quick and meaningful information when hiring someone to work in the company's plants. Once you've established contact with the reference, it takes only about five or ten minutes to get this basic information.

Written Reports

The Appendix contains sample written reports. There are three suggested report formats.

1. The *long report* is used when a client needs to review exactly what was said by each reference. It is appropriate when there are complicated circumstances or when serious negative observations have been made about the job candidate that should be recorded and analyzed.
2. The *summary report* saves time in preparing and reading, and is appropriate when the information received about the applicant is very positive and consistent, thus making a detailed elaboration of what was said by each reference unnecessary.
3. The *memo report* can be used when the information is favorable and only a brief explanation and record is needed to indicate that the necessary background review was done.

13

Handling the Rejected Applicant

Saying the right thing to a rejected applicant is critical. I believe that employment rejection is a special and very misunderstood subject that should be examined more thoroughly. In my many years in the employment business, I have seen more confusion on how to handle the rejected applicant than on any other aspect of the employment process.

All too often, because we don't want to hurt the job applicant's feelings, we try to sugarcoat the rejection in the hope that we will both feel better about the whole situation. However, with this new system of having the candidate contact and set up the reference calls, it may be very obvious why you rejected someone after you have spoken with his or her references. The applicant will surmise that he apparently did not make it because of what the references said, and may even want to know what was said about him and by whom.

When speaking with references, always reassure them that whatever they say will be treated as confidential information. It's your duty to protect your sources of information. You have an obligation to keep this information under virtual lock and key.

Before looking at the rejected finalist, let's look at another problem that also needs addressing—how to advise candidates, after you have interviewed them, that they are no longer con-

tenders for the job opening. Many interviewers
will tell all the candidates that they are in the running and thus keep everyone up in the air. The
problem with this nice-guy technique (which is a
form of avoidance) is that some applicants will
take this to mean that they are viable candidates,
falsely get their hopes up, and sometimes even
quit interviewing with other employers. To avoid
this, I suggest that you advise the candidate in
whom you no longer have an interest along these
lines: "You are a fine candidate and we appreciate
your taking the time to talk with us. But we are
talking with other qualified people and you
should continue your interviewing activity."

Above all, always let the applicant leave the
interview feeling positive about your company.
Looking for a job is never easy, so make the visit
with you as painless and pleasant as possible.
Whatever you do, treat the applicant with respect.

Then there is the applicant who knows that
he was a finalist, but for whatever reason—sometimes bad references—failed to get the job. Never
divulge or try to explain the factors that went into
your decision, because you probably don't know
all of them yourself. Above all, never tell the candidate that your decision was the result of derog-
atory information received from references. This
would be both dangerous and unnecessary. Do
yourself and the candidate a favor: Get on with
your business, and let the candidate get on with
his life. I suggest that you advise the finalist in
whom you no longer have an interest along these
lines: "It was very, very close, and certainly a difficult decision for us to make, but we decided that
another candidate met our needs more closely at
this time." Do not, under any circumstances, go

beyond this basic explanation. In fact, just keep repeating it to the job candidate as often as you need to.

File your reference notes and reports separately. A personnel record should not include employee references supplied to an employer if the identity of the person making the reference would be disclosed. In fact, I recommend destroying all your reference notes after you have made your hiring decision. You can have a perfectly innocent document, but in the hands of a skillful investigator or attorney, it can be made to look sinister. If you aren't required by law to keep a record, then get rid of it.

Believe me, if you are ever tempted to violate these rules, as I have on occasion during my career (in the belief that I was being helpful), by telling someone in pretty specific terms why he or she didn't get the job, you should think twice about going beyond what I recommend. If you don't follow my simple advice, you may end up spending weeks defending yourself, your company, and even your references from the complex inquisition of a rejected job candidate. When it's all over, no one has gained from it—especially the candidate.

My favorite story in this regard comes from a participant in one of my seminars on reference checking. A job candidate asked why he didn't get the job after everything and everybody seemed to be going his way, as far as he could tell. He was told by the employment manager that everyone liked him except the president of the company, who was not impressed and told them not to hire him. After hearing this, the candidate immediately insisted on seeing the president, causing much disruption and embarrassment in the process. As a result of this poor handling of an employment rejection, both the vice president of human resources and the employment manager were terminated by the company within the next three months.

When I was a plant manager in California, I recall an incident where two plant engineers got into hot water because they promised a job to a friend of theirs. We were looking for a new project engineer, and two of the current engineers had recommended a close friend who had recently lost his job due to large cutbacks in the aerospace industry. There were numerous engineers looking for work at the time, but these two had promised their friend that he would be the one hired for the plant position. They had gone so far as to brief him extensively about the plant, the job, and the salary they thought he would receive. However, plant and company management decided not to hire this individual because he would probably return to an aerospace position when the first opportunity arose. I had to explain to the candidate that his close friends were not the final decision makers on this matter and the job would not go to him. He was confused, upset, and very hurt. The two plant engineers were verbally reprimanded for their poor insight and judgment, which certainly did not help their career in the company.

Again, if you're involved in hiring people, and want to be good at it, you had better learn how to handle the rejected applicant. I don't think there is any area where a real pro and an unprepared amateur (however well-intentioned) become so apparent.

Part IV Summary:

Use the right questions and techniques and you will get good results. In Part IV you learned that:

▶ People basically want to help another person get a new job.

▶ Most people will be totally honest about someone they know or have worked with.

▶ It is up to you to ask the right questions in order to get correct and insightful information about someone you may hire.

▶ You have to recognize the personal needs and concerns of all the references you contact in order to get their full cooperation and honesty in providing you with the information you need.

▶ To really find what you want, you must be politely persistent and skillful in making reference contacts.

▶ In view of these considerations, it is your responsibility as a reference checker to use the right techniques and questions to get the information you need to make a smart hiring decision.

Part V

Our Obligation to Weed Out Undesirable Candidates

14

It's Time for Applied Creativity

We need to do a better job of identifying and weeding out undesirable job candidates. In this book I've described some of the things I've learned in more than thirty years of hiring people. I have tried to bring some useful insights to the subject of screening applicants. Times have changed and job candidates are no longer as honest as they used to be. It's time for applied creativity—that is, creativity that "rolls up its sleeves and gets to work." Creativity can lead to quantum leaps in improving the hiring process, a process that hasn't changed substantially over the years. Used properly, the new techniques described in these pages can produce real gains for employers trying to hire the right people.

I'm sure you will agree by now that it is more important than ever to check candidates' references. It is necessary and proper to validate through others what applicants believe or say about themselves. Only by talking in depth to those individuals who have been closely associated with the candidates is a true evaluation possible. Background information about applicants is necessary for a smart hiring decision.

The recruitment process can be long and time-consuming, depending on the level of the opening to be filled. In a typical recruiting effort, about 25 percent of the time is spent on searching for candidates; about 30 percent on screening replies and résumés; 35 percent on interviewing; and at least 10 percent (ideally) on checking references. That's a full hiring sequence, and making it a winning process requires both application and creativity.

From my observation, most people try to defend what they're doing rather than change their habits. That's why change takes place so slowly, if at all.

Networking

I can't emphasize too greatly the value of networking when checking out job candidates. A large company with which I am familiar hired a top-level research executive who was offered an elaborate employment contract, costly relocation provisions, and other expensive perks to get him to change jobs. After he had been on the new job a short time, it became clear that he was not working out. He had severe personality problems and was in over his head professionally. He was obviously a poor choice, and everyone wondered how this could have happened. Finally, the chairman of the new company called his counterpart, the chairman of the man's former company. He was quickly told that the individual had been slipping badly for several years, quite noticeably in his last few months, and, in fact, was about to be terminated when the new company hired him. The chairman of the former company went on to say, "We couldn't believe it when we heard you were hiring him," adding, "We were glad to see it because you solved a big problem for us and saved us a lot of money." He went on to tell the chairman of the new company that he would have been glad to tell someone in the proper position what was going on, but was never contacted. Well, the company chairman called in the appropriate staff members and told them the story, wanting to know why no effort had been made to contact the former employer. To make a long story short, the vice president of human resources was reprimanded and shortly thereafter resigned, while the director of professional staffing was fired. There just was no excuse for making an important and costly company decision without doing the necessary background review.

More and more companies are networking with each other regarding the hiring of people. Why fly by the seat of your pants when there is someone like yourself you can contact at another employer? I guarantee that in most cases, even though you have never met the person with whom you are speaking, that person will tell you everything you want to know about someone you are about to hire. If you're not networking to fill yourself in on the backgrounds of potential employees, you are missing the boat.

As one of my seminar participants said to the group: "We are in a war with each other for no good reason." Another member of the group added, "Yes, let's stop it now, for the good of our own companies and those fine people who need a job."

A special word for human resources people: Every one of you has a counterpart at every company for which a job applicant has ever worked. Why not call that individual and ask for information, perhaps off the record, about the candidate? It will work in the vast majority of cases. Yet very few of you will do this. It's time for the human resources function to be bolder and more results-oriented, instead of trying to invent reasons or procedures to keep something from working.

One of the reasons I wrote this book is that human resources managers have botched this subject so badly. In my view, they would have done themselves a far greater service had they figured out sensible ways to exchange job performance data with each other about current or past employees than they did by devising ingenious ways to get this information in the absence of such networking.

Does Checking References Pay Off?

Attracting and hiring the best workers is crucial to building your management team. If you don't hire the right people, it will directly effect your productivity and bottom line.

A company with which I am familiar started checking references on all job candidates before hiring them. It kept records for a full year, before and after checking references, with the following results:

	Control Year	2nd Year*
Number of candidates interviewed	168	153
Number of finalists	44	38
Number of reference checks completed	0	38
Number hired	29	22
Number hired who then left the company	16	2

*After reference checks had been instituted.

Did this pay off? You bet it did! The company had a much higher-caliber work force and a greatly reduced turnover. It also had better production figures and less friction among employees and, in the long run, had to spend far less time hiring new people.

Good hiring becomes self-perpetuating because your own employees will refer their friends to your company. Good people know other good people, just as bad people know other bad people. Hiring the right people will make your company a winner all the way around. Reference checking pays . . . and pays . . . and pays.

Pre-employment reference checking should be seen as an aggressive, proactive way to reduce turnover and build a high-quality work force. It is more than simply a way to limit legal liability. It can have a great impact on the bottom line.

Improving Performance in Your Organization

Sometimes I think we have lost sight of the practical side of hiring people. There really is no substitute for common sense when picking the right person for your organization, and I suspect most executives would agree with me. Is checking the background of a candidate a good investment? Imagine the trouble it takes to fire someone who doesn't work out. This makes the up-front investment look quite smart. Let the good ones come to work for you and the bad ones work for your competitor! You can win the hiring game by using common sense and by creatively using the effective reference checking techniques outlined in this book.

From my own experience and talking with others, the 80/20 rule applies to virtually every organization, as follows:

THE 80/20 RULE

Eighty percent of your problems come from 20 percent of your employees.

SO

One-fifth of those you hire will cause most of your future difficulties.

THEREFORE

It makes sense to identify who they are—and then not hire them.

Probably the biggest single mistake a manager can make is a bad hire. And yet they're made all the time. However, an effective pre-employment screening program can reduce hiring mistakes significantly. Probably, 75 percent or more of all hiring mistakes can be prevented through proper background checks.

An employee's past is a look into a company's future. A thorough review of a potential hire's history will give you the blueprint you need to gauge that individual's future performance. If history repeats itself, then choose your history carefully. Careful reference checking can uncover patterns of behavior that won't show up on an application form, a résumé, or an interview.

You will build a far better work force if you follow the ideas discussed in this book. Exhibit 14-1 summarizes the principal lessons taught here. Follow these points carefully to build a trouble-free work force. Don't let your learning lead to knowledge alone. Let your learning lead to action.

Exhibit 14-1. Building a trouble-free work force.

ASSUMPTIONS

The chances are overwhelming that a person will not perform any better or work any harder, or behave differently for you than he/she has for others in the past.

Eighty percent of your problems will come from 20 percent of the people you hire.

You should not hire anyone who has been a problem for someone else.

FINDING THE RIGHT EMPLOYEE

Decide to validate that what you have been led to believe about a candidate is, in fact, true and accurate (the key).

Announce to each candidate that *total honestly is expected* and that references will be checked (scare tactic).

Ask probing questions during the interview (check honesty). *Identify by name* the key people (above/same level/below) in the candidate's work life (develop references).

Tell the candidate to have certain references you have selected call you, or to set on exact time for you to call them (save time and effort).

Question references and diligently verify the information you have received. They will tell you, or at least signal to you, whether the individual has been a problem to them (spot liars and troublemakers).

THE RESULT

Avoid a hiring mistake by knowing the full truth about the applicant. Start with the right people. Build a trouble-free work force.

15

Advice to Human Resources Professionals

A special word for those working in human resources departments: You're not simply managing the personnel function of your company, you're influencing your company's future. The personnel function has undergone a dramatic change over the past fifteen years, evolving from an administrative job to one of the most important areas of the business. A company's employees represent its biggest line item expense (with the largest and most regular cash flow outlay) as well as its greatest asset. Decisions in human resources can have a very positive or negative effect on the organization's success.

As we approach the twenty-first century, we must rethink the entire hiring process. This will mean exploring new alternatives. It's time for human resources professionals to do everything legal and possible to ensure that they are hiring the right people. To stay on the cutting edge—to become proactive, not reactive—with respect to tracking a person's work history is a must in today's complex and confusing world.

My special words of advice to human resources professionals are contained in Exhibit 15-1. Please read it carefully.

Exhibit 15-1. Advice to human resources professionals.

IT'S TIME TO OPEN YOUR EYES

YOUR MISSION

▶ Become a business partner with your company's other departments.
▶ Understand their problems and needs, and actually feel the pulse of their operations.

DO THIS

▶ Play a key role in corporate performance. Develop solutions that are beneficial both to the business and to its employees.
▶ Be willing to change, despite the risk involved.
▶ Stay relevant. Become an influential force in the company's decision-making process.
▶ Be more than an administrative arm. See and respond to the strategic needs of your company.

NOT THIS

▶ Do not be complacent about or too comfortable with what's been done in the past. Don't continue using outdated methods.
▶ Don't place your policies and procedures above good business and common sense.
▶ Don't let demographics or civil rights legislation be the reason for business failure.
▶ Never let your sense of purpose become just processing paper.

Appendix

Exhibit A-1. Sample long report.

CONFIDENTIAL

TO: Great Basin Mining Corporation
3896 West Mountain Road
Provo, Utah 84604

ATTENTION: Ms. Carol J. Hyster

CANDIDATE: Mr. Alan W. Copeland

REFERENCE REPORT

Between March 4 and March 8, 1998, I spoke with the following people regarding the candidate. These parties were told that the information they provided would be treated confidentially. The references contacted and their general observations and comments were as follows:

PROFESSIONAL

1. *Mr. Kenneth Lowty, Manager Technologies, Central West Mining Corporation, Denver, Colorado*

   Mr. Lowry has known Mr. Copeland for the past twelve years at the company. He was a plant

<u>CONFIDENTIAL</u>

manager and Copeland's direct supervisor for approximately six years at the Beaver Creek Mine.

He said that Copeland is certainly a strong manager "who is able to get a lot out of his people." Copeland supervised up to 120 employees at the company and, in his opinion, was a highly effective leader and supervisor. He said Copeland is excellent at working with people. Overall he rated Copeland as a "7–8" on a scale of 10 (10 being high) compared to other production managers within the company.

He pointed out that Copeland is "a very serious-minded person" who is willing to work hard and tries to accomplish a lot in his job. If he had any criticism, it would be that Copeland sometimes tends to take on too many duties and responsibilities, which places him under a great amount of stress. However, he did point out that Copeland is able to handle a heavy workload and pressure very well. He said that "Copeland is a person who is as honest as the day is long" and does not have any serious personal problems or bad habits that ever interfered with his job performance.

He explained that over the years Copeland has become more competent in his field. He believes supervision is Copeland's strongest suit, and is where he should be assigned. If he had any recommendation for Copeland, it would be to possibly pace himself a little better in order not to be overwhelmed by the work he wants to accomplish. He felt that the best way to work with Copeland is to support him in every way, pointing out that Copeland likes some feedback regarding his progress.

He explained that Copeland is now assigned to their Warren, Montana, location under a plant

<u>CONFIDENTIAL</u>

manager who is considered to be an extremely difficult person to work for. He is aware from conversations with Copeland that Copeland has had enough of the situation and is actively pursuing other employment opportunities, commenting that he does not blame him for doing so.

2. *Mr. James Murphy, Senior Metallurgist, Central West Mining Corporation, Denver Colorado*

Mr. Murphy has known Mr. Copeland since they worked together at the Beaver Creek Mine from 1989 through 1994. He reported to Copeland for about a one-year period during that time.

He said "Copeland certainly has good skills" and is a very effective supervisor for the company. Copeland works hard, solves problems, and has a reputation for getting the job done. He also commented that Copeland is a very safety-minded manager. He explained that Copeland had responsibility for anywhere from twelve to fifty people with the company and is considered to be an effective leader, noting that Copeland is a friendly person who gets along well with everyone at all levels.

In his view, Copeland is a very dedicated and self-motivated individual who always tries to do his very best. He commented that Copeland is not as technically strong as some other management members who have an engineering degree, but Copeland certainly has a sound technical understanding. If he had any comment about Copeland it would be that Copeland could be a little more forceful at times. In his opinion, Copeland is an honest individual with strong personal standards who is always on the job putting in more time than is required.

Over the years he has watched Copeland improve his technical ability and people skills. He feels Copeland is probably a better production manager than an engineering staff member. If he had any recommendation for Copeland it would be to strengthen his technical background, commenting that he knows Copeland has done this, in addition to which Copeland has become quite knowledgeable in computerization. In his opinion, the best way to work with Copeland is to spell out his role clearly and then let him alone to do the job. He does feel Copeland likes recognition for the job he is doing and works best when this is given to him. Without question he would recommend Copeland to a new employer.

He knows Copeland is not happy working for his current boss at the Warren, Montana, location, explaining that he does not blame Copeland for wanting to make a change at this point in his career.

3. *Mr. John March, Supervisor of Human Relations and Safety, Warren Refining Co., Warren, Montana*

Mr. March and Mr. Copeland have been co-workers at the plant since 1989.

He explained that Copeland is a hardworking and results-oriented supervisor. Copeland is responsible for fifty or more hourly employees and has been consistently recognized and promoted within the company. He said Copeland works especially well with people, both in a union and a nonunion environment.

He commented that Copeland is a dedicated manager who always wants to do his very best. Copeland listens well, is very flexible, and can

CONFIDENTIAL

handle varied and complex situations in a plant. He believes that without question Copeland is very honest and reliable, pointing out that Copeland is always early and is usually one of the last to leave. He does not believe that Copeland has any personal problems that have ever interfered with his job performance.

He feels production supervision is the right field for Copeland and that Copeland very much enjoys being in charge of people. He felt the best way to work with Copeland is to clearly define his responsibilities and then let him alone to get the job done. He does feel that Copeland functions best when given some feedback regarding his progress on the job. Without question, he would recommend Copeland to a new employer.

He is very familiar with Copeland's current situation at the plant and understands his desire to make a job change at this time. He explained that Copeland as well as many other people at the plant do not get along well with the current plant manager. It has become a difficult situation for Copeland and, as a result, it would be best for Copeland to find a new career position. He firmly believes Copeland will be a valuable manager for a new employer.

4. *Ms. Mary Nolte, HR Representative, Briggs Copper Company, Tucson, Arizona*

Ms. Nolte acknowledged that Mr. Copeland was a production supervisor at the company from June 1984 to July 1989. She said that his record indicated that he was an effective and promotable employee who left to take a new job.

<u>CONFIDENTIAL</u>

EDUCATION

5. *Ms. Linda Lester, Recorder, University of Texas at Dallas*

   Ms. Lester verified that Mr. Copeland received a Bachelor's Degree in General Engineering from the university in May 1984. She is not permitted to release information about a student's grades or campus activities.

SUMMARY

During the above background review, I verified Mr. Copeland's work history and attempted to detect any possible problem areas. Based on these conversations, the following facts and conclusions can be drawn:

   A. Mr. Copeland is considered to be a knowledgeable, hardworking, and effective production supervisor.

   B. He is very good at working with people; in fact, this was described as his greatest management strength.

   C. He may not have the heavy technical background required for some positions in the industry.

   D. He is a very dedicated, serious-minded, and self-motivated individual who is willing to take on a large amount of work. Comments were made that he sometimes takes on more than he may reasonably be able to handle.

   E. All the references agreed that production management is something he enjoys and is certainly the right field for him.

CONFIDENTIAL

F. He currently reports to a boss who has a reputation for being difficult to work for. As a result, he feels it would be best to find a new career position at this time. The people spoken with who knew of his current situation agreed that his reason for leaving is valid and thought he would personally be better off working for a new employer.

G. All the references thought highly of him as a production supervisor in the metals processing industry and do recommend him to a new employer.

Compiled by: William P. Lane   Date: March 12, 1998

Exhibit A-2. Sample summary report.

CONFIDENTIAL

TO: Roswell Corporation
            1201 South Lackland
            Dayton, Ohio 45401

ATTENTION: Mr. Albert W. Johnson

CANDIDATE: Ms. Regina A. Everly

REFERENCES CONTACTED

Between April 9 and April 14, 1998, I spoke with the following people regarding the candidate. These parties were told that the information they provided would be treated confidentially.

1. Mr. Matthew Woods, OEM Sales Manager, Compra Systems, Inc., Boston, Massachusetts.
2. Ms. Wilma Kentwell, Sales Manager, Blake Palmer Company, Latrope, Pennsylvania
3. Dr. James Smith, Dean, Graduate School of Business, New Brighton College, Concord, New Hampshire
4. Mr. Charles Matson, Regional Sales Manager, Parac Industrial Co., Bedford, Massachusetts
5. Ms. Joan Davis, Clerk, Western Michigan State University, Springfield

SUMMARY OF FINDINGS

During the above background review, I verified the candidate's work history and attempted to detect any possible problem areas. Based on these conversations, the following facts and conclusions can be drawn:

<u>CONFIDENTIAL</u>

<u>PROFESSIONAL</u>

A. Ms. Everly was described as a very experienced, hardworking, and highly competent sales representative. She has consistently ranked at the very top of the sales force with her current employer, normally being either first or second in standing among their sales representatives.

B. She is considered to be a very self-motivated and self-driven individual who is determined to be successful and will do whatever is necessary to be a top sales performer. She has an excellent sales background and has always performed in an exemplary manner.

C. She is very thorough and does excellent follow-up work with her customers. She gains their respect and confidence, which is considered to be one of the reasons for her high level of success.

D. She was described as a very likable and personable individual who gets along quite well with people at all levels. Although she is aggressive, she does not intimidate or irritate people and is, therefore, able to get their support and commitment.

E. She is a part-time college teacher who always receives top ratings from her students. It was noted that she is always helpful and willing to take extra steps to assist students.

<u>PERSONAL</u>

F. Ms. Everly is a very positive, aggressive, and determined individual who is fully committed to reaching her personal goals.

<u>CONFIDENTIAL</u>

G. Everyone spoken with felt that she is a totally honest and reliable person who can always be counted on to give her very best effort.

H. Comments were made that if she has any weakness, it would be that she sometimes works too hard and is something of a perfectionist.

I. It was pointed out that she really does want to help people and will literally go out of her way to assist someone because she receives a great amount of personal satisfaction from doing this.

J. She is very money-motivated and wants to be financially successful. In fact, she is continually exploring new ways to increase her earnings.

K. Everyone commented that she is also a good wife and mother. One reference noted that she has two loves in her life, her job and her family.

L. She has never had any serious personal problems or bad habits that interfered with her job performance.

M. She received an M.B.A. degree from Western Michigan State University in 1984, as stated on her résumé.

<u>OVERALL</u>

N. The references feel that Ms. Everly has been maturing and growing as a businesswoman and sales representative. She is continually improving her skills and abilities.

O. There was no question in anyone's mind that selling is the right field for her and that she really loves this activity. A number of comments were made that she is the type of individual who probably does not want and should not be placed in

CONFIDENTIAL

sales management because she seems to thrive and excel as a field salesperson.

P.   A comment was made that she can be impatient at times and needs to understand the limits of the team that supports her. Although this is not a serious problem, she does move so fast on her own that sometimes the support she needs has difficulty keeping up with her.

Q.   It was suggested that the best way to work with her is to continually add new responsibilities and goals for her.

R.   She is quite community-minded and has heavy involvements outside of work. She thrives on activity and success and needs this kind of stimulation in her life.

S.   Compra (her current employer) is apparently going through considerable problems and facing a possible downsizing, so she is willing to make a job change because of the great uncertainty in the company, especially if the new job offers more income potential.

T.   Comments were made that she is the kind of person who needs a minimum amount of direction; however, she does like and appreciates recognition. It seems important to her to be recognized for the high standing she has within her company.

U.   Ms. Everly appears to be an exemplary person and a strong candidate for account management responsibility. The references believe that she is an outstanding candidate for a sales position.

Prepared by: Susan T. Wylie   Date: April 16, 1998

Exhibit A-3. Sample memo report.
_____

CONFIDENTIAL

TO: Ms. Patricia Hendricks
               Apex Company
               Fax No. 316-644-2248

CANDIDATE: Mr. Kenneth Adams

On April 30–May 1, 1998, I spoke with the following
people regarding the candidate: *James McCoy,* Chief
Engineer, Manson, Inc.; *David Blatner,* Manufacturing
Manager, Kerr Corp.; *Peter Jones,* Project Engineer, Jones
Engineering; and *Sam Malroy,* Service Manager, Bell
Honda, Inc.

The references described him as a very smart, conscien-
tious, and hardworking mechanical designer who is doing
an excellent job with his current employer. He is a self-
starter and works very well on his own. He is the kind of
person who can see alternative ways to approach a problem and is not afraid to try new ways. He is very proficient
in CAD CAM and three-dimensional models and knows
unigraphics very well. He gets along well with everyone,
is a good team player, and was rated as a superior performer in his current role.

The references said that he is a pleasant person who has
a somewhat "down-home" manner about him. He communicates well, especially when speaking, and has a witty
way of expressing himself. One reference commented
that he works almost too hard and needs to slow down. If
there was any recommendation for him it was that he
needs more formal education. He is considered to be a
very honest and reliable individual who has never had any

<u>CONFIDENTIAL</u>

serious personal problems or bad habits that interfered with his job performance, although one reference mentioned that "he does chew tobacco."

The references thought engineering design and NC Programming is where he belongs. It was recommended that the best way to work with him is to define his job and then let him run with it. He requires a minimum amount of direction and supervision.

All the references believe Mr. Adams will be a definite asset wherever he is employed. His current employer said that it will be a big loss if he leaves them.

Compiled by: Joseph R. Sanders   Date: May 6, 1998

Index